New Plays for Mature Actors

An Anthology

edited by Bonnie L. Vorenberg

Morton Grove, Illinois U.S.A.

Other titles from Coach House Press, Inc.

ACTING UP! An Innovative Approach to Creative Drama for Older Adults

Library of Congress Cataloging in Publication Data
Vorenberg, Bonnie L., ed.
 New Plays for Mature Actors
  CONTENTS: Anna's Brooklyn Promise. — The Day They Kidnapped Blanche.
— Lalapalooza Bird. — [etc.]
  I. Senior adult plays.

Library of Congress
 Card Catalog Number: 86-072782
ISBN 0-88020-131-2

Book and cover design by Rhoda Sterling,
Sterling Graphics and Communication

Cover photos: Howard Amend, Ivy Margaret Wharton, Jeanne Jenkins,
 Arts for Elders and *Oregon Senior Theatre Ensemble*

Contents

Foreword

Older Americans are discovering the theatre in ever-increasing numbers! A recent Harris survey reports that attendance at live theatre performances by persons more than age 65 rose fifteen percent in the past three years. But even more significant and more exciting are the increased numbers of older adults who are joining adult theatre troupes as actors and technicians. For them, *New Plays for Mature Actors*, as the first anthology in the field, will fill an enormous need! Bonnie Vorenberg, *Arts for Elders* and the Oregon Senior Theatre Ensemble, should be heartily congratulated for this welcome contribution.

The nation's older citizens bring to the performing arts a lifetime rich in human experience. In six or more decades of living, they witness world-shaking events and ride personal roller coasters of joy, sadness, suffering, good fortune and adversity that are quintessential theatre. What better vehicle than the stage for the dramatization of their special insights. The ten plays in this anthology offer a variety of excellent roles to older performers and, by their subject matter, demonstrate possibilities for expanded horizons in late life. If school children see the plays, it may make a real difference in their concepts of aging now in in the years to come.

Since its inception in 1973, the National Center on Arts and the Aging, a program of The National Council on the Aging (NCOA), in partnership with the National Endowment for the Arts, has recognized the boundless capacity of older adults for contributing to the nation's cultural and creative mosaic and has worked successfully to forge a close relationship between the fields of arts and aging. We have watched the stage productions of older actors grow from vaudeville shows and skits to the more professional and polished performance of senior adult troupes like the Oregon Senior Theatre Ensemble. Some performing groups have moved in the direction of living history; some produce strictly issue-related plays; still others seek scripts that give range to their acting abilities and serve mainly to entertain. *New Plays for Mature Actors* will be an excellent resource for individuals and groups who sense the stirring of their creative energy in later life and turn to the theatre for its expression.

Priscilla McCutcheon
Former Director
National Center on Arts
    and the Aging, NCOA

Preface

What are the Needs?

I had spent several years of constant involvment in teaching, directing and all other aspects of senior adult theatre when I realized that there were large problems with availability of scripts for senior adult theatre. I began to listen to the needs of practitioners from all sections of the country. They repeatedly expressed the need for more plays that were specially designed to meet the needs and abilities of the senior actors with whom they worked. Specifically, they wanted ones that were shorter in length, were applicable to both classroom and staged presentations and would feature older adults in a positive image.

In response to these needs I chaired two nationwide play searches under the umbrella of my membership on the American Theatre Association's Senior Adult Theatre Committee. Hundreds of scripts from playwrights and publishers were read and evaluated. Forty-five of the best were chosen to appear on the 1982 and 1983 "New Play List for Senior Adult Theatre".

But the "New Play Lists" were not enough. Practitioners expressed frustration with having to write individual letters to find out more about each play. They wanted one useful volume that would include several first-rate works. Their demand evolved into *New Plays for Mature Actors*.

Many other factors indicate a growing need for anthologies of *New Plays for Mature Actors* in the future. In recent years, the field of senior adult theatre has begun to grow at an encouraging rate! There is great expansion in amount, style and quality of work being done. By all indications, the field will continue to expand in order to accomodate the large increase of older citizens that demographic studies predict so vividly.

This quickly growing population group foreshadows other changes. As the number of productive years increase, so will the average senior adult's health, vitality and thus, their happiness. Our generation will exceed the capabilities of prior generations to live long and productive lives. As these changes occur, we will continue to disprove the many myths that surround aging. American societies will develop new concepts of what it means to grow older.

The greater number of vital years will see some elders carrying greater income, more education and more life-long capacity to practice and enjoy the arts far into their later years. This visable, energetic corps of senior adults will create greater opportunities for themselves to share the challenge, stimulation and fun that theatre can provide.

Who Can Use These Scripts?

This collection will be useful for professionals and volunteers who work with the entire spectrum of people over 55: from fit and fiesty to those who are frail. Activity directors, senior center personnel, theatre practitioners, recreation specialists, therapists and volunteers can locate valuable material here. Those who work in nursing homes, retirement homes, day care, community college or other settings will find scripts that are applicable to their clientele.

About the Scripts

The plays were selected because they portray characters who use charm and a great deal of insight to tackle life's many complexities. They:

- reflect a positive image of aging,
- feature a majority of women's roles,
- are either useful, shorter scripts or inspiring, longer works,
- are adaptable for classroom work or complete, fully mounted staged productions,
- provide opportunities for beginning actors and actresses along with challenges for more advanced performers,
- require simple sets, costumes, props and other production elements,
- have a good sense of logic to aid with memorization,
- can be used in all geographic areas.

What about Royalty?

Most of the scripts require a modest royalty payment for performances, usually in the range of $5 to $25. This variable fee for other-than-classroom use is due even if no admission is charged. The royalty is one of the small ways to reward the playwright for the great amount of time and work dedicated to providing directors and actors with a good script.

Royalty waivers are issued in a few instances; they would be available from the controlling agent who is noted behind the title page of each play.

Some Thank Yous

This collection would not have been possible without the untiring work of the play reading committee. We are also indebted to the playwrights for courageously sharing their vision and insight into the lives of older adults. Together, we value David Jewell, a publisher who has advanced senior adult theatre by making new materials available and accessible.

Personally, the work of several individuals has made this collection a reality; the encouragement of Pauline Peotter, the assistance of Irene Phoenix and the faithful support of Robert Dupuy.

My inspiration comes from the many students, performers and supporters who are involved in my *Arts for Elders* program in the Oregon Senior Theatre Ensemble. They convince me of the value of work in senior adult theatre when time and time again, they demonstrate how life can be full of *life* at any and every age.

Bonnie L. Vorenberg, editor
March, 1986

Anna's Brooklyn Promise
by D. K. Oklahoma

Anna's Brooklyn Promise

by D. K. Oklahoma

Cast List

Anna	Jack
Virginia	Roscoe
Bea	

2

Anna's Brooklyn Promise

by D. K. Oklahoma

ACT ONE, SCENE ONE

At rise: Jack is working behind the counter, getting ready for the dinner hour. The wall clock reads 3:21.

Anna and Virginia are seated across from each other at the center booth, with Anna facing the restroom door. Purses and shopping bags are piled beside them on the benches, cups and saucers on the table. They are in the midst of a good gossip.

Virginia: She says forty. My son says forty. Her driver's license says forty-three. *(more loudly, to Jack)* Mr. Moore, could I have a little more hot water over here, if it's not too much trouble.

Anna: *(to Jack)* Me, too . . . while you're at it. *(Both ladies quickly and noisily sip at their cups to finish up what they have before Jack arrives with more hot water.)*

Jack: *(filling the cups)* Did you ladies have a good day uptown?

Virginia: *(nods)* We were shopping for a wedding present.

Anna: Her nephew, Richard is getting married.

Jack: Is that right? Well, that's good. Nice day for it. You know, it's real nice to see you in here again, Miz Kranze. You don't get out much these days.

Anna: No . . .

Virginia: You tell her, Mr. Moore. I've talked myself blue in the face. It's all I can do to pry her out once a month to do a little shopping. Get out with people, I tell her . . . . but does she listen? Of course not. She's like my daughter-in-law. . . .

Jack: *(to Anna)* I remember you and Mr. Kranze, may he rest in peace, usta come in here a lot. For the plate lunch special. He was a nice man. I miss seeing him.

Anna: Me too, yes.

Jack: He always enjoyed my meatloaf.

Virginia: *(firmly)* Yes, Mr. Moore, but that's all in the past. *(meaningfully)* We have to think about now. . . and the future. Don't you agree, Mr. Moore?

3

Jack: *(misses the point)* A nice man. He always usta love my brown gravy. . .

> *(Anna turns away from the conversation, toward the audience, trying not to cry, with only moderate success. Jack is oblivious to her discomfort, despite Virginia's facial expressions to warn him off the subject.)*

Virginia: *(trying to change the subject)* I never cared for gravy dishes, spaghetti's my favorite. . . don't you agree, Anna?

Anna: *(trying to pull herself together)* W-With m-meat sauce?

Virginia: I prefer meatballs. About the size of a skinny golf ball. *(makes a gesture toward Jack to tell him to "go away." Anna doesn't see this. Jack finally gets the idea and retreats behind the counter.)*

> *The outside door opens and BEA enters. She looks around, confused, as if she doesn't kown just where she is. BEA is carrying two pillow cases filled with lumpy things and a paper shopping bag with handles. Her coat is open to reveal a printed cotton housedress. She is wearing sunglasses, white anklets and one red slipper. The other slipper sticks out of her open purse, which dangles on one arm. She is hatless and her hair is untidy. Bea sits on the empty bench at the other table, her back to Virginia.*

> *The two other women take in her appearance (although Bea is seemingly unaware of them) and give each other glances of mutual disapproval and surprise.*

Jack: *(to Bea)* Wanna see a menu?

Bea: *(dazed)* Well . . . I'm not sure . . . .

Jack: It's a little early for supper, but I can fix you a sandwich or any of the breakfast stuff on the back.

Bea: Well I'm very hungry. I didn't eat my lunch. It was fish and she knows I hate fish, so she always fixes it, and I just couldn't . . . *(falters to a halt and seems to lose track of what she is saying. She has forgotton that Jack is standing there. She realizes her slipper is in her purse, takes it out and looks at it, then slips it on her foot without explanation. Then she remembers Jack, gives a little jump)* Oh!

Jack: *(waiting patiently, unaware of her little lapse)* Maybe something to drink?

Bea: Oh . . . yes, that sounds very nice. I would like to have a coke or something. *(clutches her purse nervously)* But I have a little problem. *(opens and then closes the purse absentmindedly)* I had to give the cab driver all most all my money. Do you take checks?

Jack: Sorry.

Bea: I thought not. Neither would he. That's why I had to give him all my money. She never let me have much cash. I only had eleven dollars. *(The other two women are listening to all this, growing more and more curious, but trying not to be obvious.)* It was a nine dollar ride, and then, of course, there was the tip. I always believe in tipping, don't you?

Jack: I certainly do.

Bea: *(opens her hand to study some coins)* So now I only have twenty-three cents. Do you have anything for twenty cents, since you won't take a check?

Jack: Twenty cents?

Bea: How about a cup of tea? Is that enough for a tea?

Jack: Tea's sixty-five.

Bea: Oh. *(Virginia turns around, clears her throat meaningfully and glares at Jack, shaming him with her eyes.)*

Jack: *(gives in)* Oh, what the hell. Sure you can have a cup of tea for twenty cents. . . just this once. *(gives Virginia a "I hope you're satisfied" look)* . . .but no lemon!

Bea: Oh, I don't use it, anyway. That's very nice of you. I'll be sure to pay you back . . . just as soon as I get my check cashed. I promise.
(Jack goes to get the tea, etc.)

Virginia, smitten with curiosity turns to study Bea more closely. She wiggles her own fingers to call Anna's attention to Bea's diamond rings. Bea does not notice this.

Jack: *(pulls a tea bag out of his pocket, drops it in Bea's cup, pours the water)* There you go. A nice cup of tea.

Bea: Thank you so much. I won't forget your kindness.

Jack: *(eyeing the bundles)* 'Cuse me for askin', lady, I don't mean to be nosy, but was you in a fire, or somethin'? It almost looks like you was in a hurry to leave someplace or somethin'. . . .

Bea: Oh, no, that's all right. *(hesitates, looking at her lumpy bundles as if seeing them for the first time)* I can see why you would think that . . . *(seems to make up her mind about something)* . . . . yes! You are exactly right. I was in a fire. I just grabbed what I could and got out. *(her voice trails off)* Just what I could carry . . . .

Jack: Gee, that's a damn shame. *(He is now a little uncomfortable. . . . why did he get involved? He shrugs at Anna and Virginia.)* Well, enjoy your tea. *(He returns to the kitchen.)*

Virginia: *(leans over to peek under the bench at Bea's feet and stage whispers to Anna)* She's wearing house slippers!

Bea: *(unaware of the other women, to Jack)* I hate to be so much trouble, but do you have a ladies room?

Jack: *(points)* Right over there. Help yourself.

Bea: *(starts to get up, gathering up her bundles)* Don't take away my tea.

Jack: Say, I'm afraid you won't be able to take that stuff in there with you. That's where I store my cleaning stuff. There's just enough room to turn around.

Bea: *(distressed)* Oh dear.

Jack: Don't worry. I'll keep an eye on it for you. . . or maybe Miz Brodzienski and Miz Kranze will. It'll be all right. Not many in here this time a day.

Bea: *(hesitates)* This is everything I have in the world. . . .

Virginia: *(smiles reassuringly)* We'll look after it for you.

Bea: *(still uncertain)* If you're sure it's no trouble. . .

Jack: No problem.

Bea: All right, I'll be right back. Thank you. *(exits)*

> *Virginia hesitates only a second and then turns, leans over the back of the bench and swiftly opens the top of one pillow case and peers inside.*

Anna: *(shocked)* VIRGINIA! What are you doing?

Virginia: *(digging in the bag, stage whispers)* I'm just checking. How do we know she didn't steal these things?

Jack: *(upset by Virginia's action)* She didn't look like no thief to me.

Anna: I don't t-t-think we should get involved. . .

Virginia: She's got a nice new toaster in here and a feather duster! *(holds it up)* What on earth would you save a feather duster for, if your house was on fire?

Jack: Maybe she's the tidy type. *(laughs at his own joke.)*

Anna: *(alarmed)* I - I think you should stop! It's none of our business.

Virginia: Aren't you curious? I never saw her around here before. I wonder who she it?

Anna: *(upset)* I n-never saw her before, either. . .

Jack: I don't know her, but I can't afford to get involved in nobody else's troubles.

Anna: P- put that stuff back. . . .

Virginia: *(holds up a mixing spoon)* Looks like she grabbed the first things she came to. . .

Anna: That's what folks d-do in a fire. Put that back!

Virginia: Here's a nice gold hand mirror. *(holds it up)*

Jack: *(now behind counter)* I don't want no part a this. All's I did was give her a cup of tea. Discount.

Virginia: Look at this lovely scarf. I saw one of these at Macy's for $35. This is no poor woman!

Anna: Maybe she's a bag lady. May-maybe she stole those things!

Virginia: That's what I said before. Maybe we should call a cop. *(holds up a potholder)* Look at this! What a crazy thing to save.

Jack: Don't call no cop. Just put that stuff back and mind your own business. It's the best way. I know.

Virginia: *(holding up a smaller sack)* What's all this? *(She shakes it, then peeks inside and gasps, reaches in and pulls out a flashy diamond bracelet.)* Could this be real? This is a whole bag full of jewelry. Diamonds! My God!

Jack: *(panics)* Now I know I don't want nuthin' to do with this. For God's sake, Miz Brodzienski, put that stuff back!

Anna: Do bag ladies have jewelry?

Virginia: *(putting things back hastily)* Who knows? They're all crazy.

Anna: Why would she carry all th-that around with her?

Virginia: I wish I didn't have to go fix Harry's supper. I'd stay around here and find out more about our rich little bag lady.

Jack: I don't know nuthin' about no bag ladies!

Anna: She seemed so . . . lost, and confused. She didn't even have enough money for a cup of tea! Maybe she really was in a fire.

Jack: I don't know nuthin' about no fires!

Virginia: Why don't you stay on here and talk to her a while, Anna? You can call me later and tell me what you find out.

Anna: *(terrified at the thought)* Oh. I c-couldn't do th-that!

Virginia: Well, I can only stay a few more minutes. *(looks at her watch)* Darn it. Harry wants his dinner early tonight. It's his bowling night. *(looks toward the restroom)* I wish she'd hurry up. I want to get another look at her before I leave.

Anna: I th-think I'll leave, too. I'm a little tired. And anyway, David always told me not to get involved with strangers.

Jack: *(moves closer to the end of the counter nearest the restroom door, listens, whispers)* I think I hear cryin'.

Virginia: *(gets up, tiptoes toward the door, listens)* She's crying her eyes out! The poor thing!

Anna: *(still seated to Virginia)* Come back. It's none of our business.

Virginia: *(sternly)* Listen, Anna Kranze, there's a human being in there, crying her eyes out. I can show a little human warmth can't I?

Anna: I think we should just leave. David always told me, don't-don't get involved.

Virginia: *(a little sharply)* I hate to be the one to tell you this, Anna, he was a nice man, but David wasn't God. You can't go back to what David said for every decision you make. *(points to the bathroom door)* I think that's a nice woman in there, and if I didn't have to hurry home to make Harry's supper, I'd try to get to the bottom of this.

Jack: I never had nobody cryin' in my john before. Do you think I should call somebody to come help her. . . or take her home or sumpthin'?

Virginia: I think we should just wait until she comes out and ask her what we can do to help.

Anna: *(shakes her head)* Oh, I don't think we should! My David. . . .

Virginia: *(cuts her off, exasperated)* Oh, for heaven's sake, Anna! She's just an old woman, in some kind of trouble. Poor thing. She's not going to hurt anyone!

Anna: *(twisting her hands)* B-but, David. . . .

Virginia: *(kindly)* Now just a minute, Anna. I don't want to sound mean, but I gotta say somethin'. Take a look at yourself. David's been gone over three years and you're still letting him run your life! You gotta start thinking for yourself. Stop all this living in the past! *(Virginia slides onto the bench beside Anna, putting her arm around the other woman)* You can't go on being afraid of life, Anna darlin'. You gotta get out of yourself. Get involved. Be with other people. You can't live your life on a monthly shopping trip with me! You're still a young woman, Anna! Let yourself go. Take a few chances!

Anna: You're a good friend, Virginia.

Virginia: I try to be, Anna. We been friends a long time.

Anna: Since Brooklyn.

Virginia: Yeah!: *(slides back onto her own side of the bench)* That was a lotta years ago.

Anna: I was always happy in Brooklyn, but Momma, she wanted to get out. I miss the old neighborhood.

Virginia: You wouldn't say that if you could see it now. Aye! You can't walk down the street without a gun! You couldn't drag me back there. No way.

Anna: I wouldn't want to. The Brooklyn I remember is still alive, in my mind's eye. I can see it so clear. Like yesterday. Those were the good old days! Do you remember the little iron balcony on our apartment? We used to sit out there for hours in the summer and talk, remember? And the way Mr. Hannaford's bakery smelled, down on the corner. Why I can remember. . . .

Virginia: Now just a minute, Anna. That's exactly what I mean! There you go again! You can't be looking back all the time. You gotta look ahead! *(turns to Jack for support)* Ain't that right, Mr. Moore?

Jack: You gotta keep up wit things! *(moves close to the women, very earnest)* Now, for instance, you look at this place. Lotsa folks only see a dumpy little diner, but I got plans. *(gestures)* I'm gonna move these booths down and put in another one by the wall and next year, give it a coat of paint. Maybe recover the benches. *(leans close to Anna)* See, it may be only a dumpy little diner, but even it's got a future, Miz Kranze. I gotta keep up with the times. Can't look back.

Virginia: That's exactly what I mean! You should take a lesson from Jack, Anna. Plan ahead. Where do you want your life to be in a few years? Next year, even? Do you still want to be living the way you are now . . . scared of everything . . . all alone?

Anna: Well . . .

Jack: Time don't wait for no one. Who's to say we'll even be alive next year ourselfs? You gotta take the bull by the horns, I say.

Anna: Oh, I – I. . . .

Virginia: *(interrupts)* Get out of the house. Take a class in something. Thank God, David left you so you don't have to work, but maybe that's not the best thing for you. You need to be with other people. Maybe you should get a job. . .

Jack: *(inappropriately)* Faint heart never won fair lady. *(realizes that this is inappropriate and tries to recover)* Well, you know what I mean. You gotta strike while the iron is hot! *(Virginia gives him a look of exasperation that he is confusing the issue. He shrugs, foolishly.)*

Virginia: You got a lot of life ahead of you, Anna.

Jack: Tempest figits. *(The women frown at Jack, aware that this doesn't sound quite right)*

Anna: *(sighs)* I guess you're right. . .

There is the faint sound of a toilet flushing.

Jack: *(nods toward the door)* I think she's coming out.

Virginia: Promise me you'll think about what I said, Anna. Promise me you'll do something about it.

Anna: I k-know you're right, Virginia. . . .

Virginia: I mean it! Make me a promise.

Anna: *(holds up her little finger, smiling shyly)* Like we used to . . . in Brooklyn?

Virginia laughs and holds up her own right hand. The two women link little fingers across the table top.

Virginia: Okay. Now promise me.

Anna: I promise I'll make a fresh start. I'll get out of myself and get involved in life. There. Is that what you want?

Virginia: *(very pleased, laughing)* That's wonderful. I'm so proud of you! *(They unlink fingers.)*

Virginia: Now, as much as I hate to. . . I've got to go. Harry turns into a bear when his supper is late. *(get up, gathers her stuff, then leans over and kisses Anna on the cheek)* Don't forget . . . *(playfully)* you can't break a Brooklyn promise!

Anna: *(smiles)* No one would dare to break a Brooklyn promise!

Virginia: You heard her, Mr. Moore. She's gonna turn over a new leaf. She promised!

Jack: I heard her!

Virginia: Now, give me a call later and let me know what you decide to do to keep the promise. I'll be dying to hear.

The restroom door opens and Bea comes out. Her hair is more tidy and she seems a little more composed. She returns to her original seat, ignoring the others. She picks up her cup, lost in her own thoughts.

Virginia: *(talking to Anna, but watching Bea)* Just one small step. It doesn't matter what you do. Just speak to someone you don't know . . . a contact . . . no matter how small. I know you can do it. *(prepares to leave, the dinner ticket in her hand)*

Anna: I'll try.

Virginia: The treat's on me, today. I'm so happy about your promise. *(Hands Jack the money)* Here you go, Mr. Moore. Keep the change . . . it's only a quarter.

Jack: Thanks, Miz Brodzienski. Every little bit helps.

Anna stands up while this is going on, staring at Bea. Anna hesitates, gathers her courage and approaches the other bench. Bea is oblivious to her presence. Anna looks over her shoulder in Virginia's direction with a "look at me now, Ma" expression on her face and leans toward Bea, extending her own hand for a handshake.

Anna: *(very awkward, all in a rush)* How d-do you do? My name is Mrs. David Kranze. I have a big apartment on 102nd Street. Would you like to come and live with me? *(Virginia makes a little choking sound and stares at Jack in horror. Oblivious to the reaction of her friends, Anna smiles down at the befuddled Bea.)* You can have the blue room.

Bea: *(blankly)* What?

Anna: Don't you need a place to stay?

Bea: *(dazed)* Well. . . yes. .

Anna: *(bravely)* Then, don't be afraid. Take a chance. You're still a young woman. You can make a fresh start. What do you say?

Bea: *(still dazed, but pleased)* Well. . . all right. . . . I will!

Anna: Good!

Virginia and Jack continue to stare at Anna, mouths agape, as the

Scene Ends

ACT ONE, SCENE TWO

Same scene, a few moments later: Bea is sipping her tea and looking through some things in her purse, still seated at the table. It's almost as if she has forgotten about Anna. Virginia has dragged Anna over to the door by the counter. Jack leans close, concern on his face. Anna is being scolded. While they talk, Bea takes a pill.

Virginia: How could you do such a thing, Anna? That woman's a complete stranger!

Jack: *(worried)* I never seen her before. We don't even know her name!

Anna: *(looking uneasily at Bea)* You said you wanted me to get involved . . . she seems like a nice person.

Virginia: *(almost hysterical, but trying not to talk too loud)* Get involved? Well, yes, of COURSE! But NOT ask her to move into your house! Whatever were you thinking of? I meant maybe say "Hello, nice weather we're having" or something like that. Not "Would you like to live with me!" My God, Anna, what on earth are you going to do now?

Anna: Well, I think I'll buy her a sandwich, I don't have any bread in the house.

Virginia: A sandwich!

Anna:: *(mildly)* She didn't eat her lunch, remember, the fish?

Jack: *(helpful)* I got some nice egg salad.

Virginia: *(patiently)* I don't think you're listening to me, Anna Kranze. You can't take a perfect stranger home with you!

Anna: Why not?

Virginia: *(upset)* Why not? Why not! *(looks at Jack for support)* She's a stranger!

Anna: But you said . . .

Jack: My corned beef is nice, too.

Virginia: *(clutches Anna's arm and hisses)* You don't even know her name!

Anna: I will, if you'll let me get back over there. I'm afraid she's going to think we're talking about her.

Virginia: I can't let you take a total stranger home with you. What if she's a criminal!

Anna: *(gently)* I don't think criminals run around in house slippers rescuing feather dusters.

Jack: And toasters. Don't forget the toaster.

Anna: My doctor's brother's wife set her kitchen on fire by accident from the grease and all she remembered to save was a box of Rice Krispies and it was half empty. People grab funny things at a time like that. *(nods wisely.)* Saved the Rice Krispies but the new blender got all burned up.

(indicates Bea) I think she's really just a poor woman whose house burned up. She needs some help . . . and *(surprised at herself)* I want to help her! I really do!

Virginia: But I feel responsible . . . . .

Anna: Well, maybe you do, but you shouldn't. Maybe it was a little sudden, but this was entirely my own idea. My heart just went out to her, even without what you said. She looked so lost. Those slippers! The poor thing.

Jack: Nobody goes around outside in house slippers without a good reason . . .

Virginia: *(doubtful)* Well . . .

Anna: I think she rushed out of her burning house and saved what little she could, just like she said. She has no place to stay. . . and I've got all that room!

Virginia: *(doubtful)* Well . . .

Anna: So I take her home for a day or two until she can get organized. What's the harm in that?

Virginia: I don't know, but . . .

Jack: I think it's a real nice thing. She don't look like a criminal or nothin' to me, either.

Anna: Jack's a good judge of character.

Jack: You gotta be, in this business.

Virginia: *(glances at her wrist watch.)* Oh, my gosh. I've got to get home. *(hesitates, still unwilling to desert her chum)* Oh, dear. I hate to leave you – – with her.

Anna: *(smiles and pats Virginia's hand)* I'll be fine. Run along and fix Harry's supper.

Virginia: You keep an eye on her, Mr. Moore.

Jack: You bet, Miz Brodzienski.

Virginia: Well, I really have to go. I'll call you right after supper, Anna.

Anna: Okay. Good-bye, dear. Don't be late . . . and don't worry!

Virginia: Good-bye. Be careful. *(kisses Anna's cheek and exits.)*

Jack: So. What'll it be? Egg salad or corned beef?

Anna: Well, I don't know – I'll have to ask her. Oh, I almost forgot; she asked me to give you this. For the tea. *(hands him some coins)*

Jack: *(surprised)* Twenty-three cents? I told her only twenty. . . this time.

Anna: *(whispers)* I think that's your tip. Three cents. It was all she had.

Jack: *(pleased)* Now ain't that nice? A tip. Imagine that, after her house burned down and all. Maybe this is going to work out all right. She's got class.

Anna smiles at him, then goes to sit down across from Bea. Bea still seems very confused. She looks a little surprised to see Anna again.

Bea: Oh . . . .

Anna: Are you hungry?

Bea: Oh. . . *(getting slightly interested)* Hungry? Well, yes, I am. She gave me fish for lunch and she knows I can't eat fish, so I didn't. So I guess I am hungry. *(picks up her handbag, opens and then closes it, frowning)* But I don't have any money yet and no one will take my checks.

Anna: I'll buy you a sandwich – – or whatever you want. You can pay me back later, if you want to.

Bea: *(overwhelmed)* Oh, how nice! *(begins to cry)* I'm sorry. I'm sorry, It's just that everything is so – so strange. I was there, and now I'm here . . .

Anna: Yes, I know. There's nothing worse than a fire . . . .

Bea: *(puzzled)* What?

Anna: Your house. the fire.

Bea: *(looks around, dazed)* Oh, yes. . . . the fire.

Anna: How did it start?

Bea: What?

Anna: The FIRE. How did it start? In the kitchen?

Bea: *(vaguely)* Uh, no. Not exactly. *(clutches Anna's arm)* Did, did you really mean that . . . what you said . . . about me coming home with you?

Anna: Of course. *(Bea begins to cry again.)* Oh dear.

Bea: *(very touched)* You're so kind. You never saw me before and you're willing to take me home.

Anna: Well, I've got plenty of room. I'm a widow and . . .

Bea: Me, too. Now.

Anna: *(stricken)* Oh. Oh dear. Was it the fire? Oh . . . maybe I shouldn't ask that. *(falters to a halt, fearful that she has offended or hurt Bea)* I didn't mean . . .

Bea: No. Not the fire. A year ago. Thirteen months. He was only seventy.

Anna: I'm sorry.

Bea: Me, too. I just haven't gotten used to the idea. We were married over forty years. You don't forget forty years in just thirteen months.

Anna: Of course not.

Bea: *(delicately)* I guess I should eat a little something.

Anna: How about an egg salad sandwich?

Bea: That sounds wonderful. On plain bread.

Anna: *(to Jack)* Jack, she'll have an egg salad – on plain bread. *(to Bea)* And another cup of tea? *(Bea nods. Anna continues to Jack.)* And some more tea, please.

Jack: Coming right up. *(starts fixing it)* Lettuce and tomato? *(Bea nods "yes".)*

Anna: You'll feel better after you eat. *(struggling for a topic)* So! *(awkward pause)* So. *(pause)* You, uh . . . don't like fish? *(another awkward pause)* Uh, me, neither.

Bea: She knows that. That's why she's always shoving it at me. It's no accident! Yesterday it was tuna. Today, haddock. I hate fish.

Anna: It smells up the house.

Bea: Once she even gave me sardines. *(shudders)* It was awful!

Anna: Excuse me, but who is this terrible person who keeps shoving the fish at you?

Bea: *(surprised that she doesn't know)* Oh! Veronica, of course, my step-son's wife. She hates me . . . . *(Bea drifts off.)*

Anna: *(prompting)* . . .And that's why she gives you fish?

Bea: Yes. *(pause)* And the other things . . . .

Anna: *(drops her own voice)* What things?

Bea: *(drops her eyes and fiddles with her purse)* Oh, I can't talk about them right now. Maybe after I eat.

Anna: *(puzzled, she lets it drop)* Well, of course. You certainly don't have to talk about it. *(pause)* If you don't want to.

Bea: *(drops back into a cautious whisper)* She wants my money.

Anna: Who?

Bea: Veronica. And my step-son.

Anna: Oh.

Bea: *(nodding wisely)* She thinks I don't know about it.

Anna: *(intrigued)* Oh?

Bea: She's been planning this for a long time. She thinks I can't fight back now that my husband's dead.

Anna: Veronica?

Bea: *(nods wisely again)* She only married him for the money. I know it.

Anna: *(trying to sort it all out)* You mean your son?

Bea: Step-son. My own son would never do such a thing. *(begins to cry again)*

Anna: Was he in the fire?

Bea: *(blankly)* Fire?

Anna: *(getting a little exasperated)* the fire. At your house. The one you just escaped from *(points to Bea's bundles)* Remember? that fire!

Bea: *(looks very uncomfortable, shifts in her seat and can't meet Anna's eyes)* Uh, there wasn't a fire. *(sighs)* Not really.

Anna: *(stunned)* What! You told me . . . .

Bea: *(waves her to silence, shaking her head)* A lie. All a lie. I had to tell you something. The fire was your idea. Well, somebody's idea. It just seemed to fit.

Jack arrives with the sandwich just as she says this, starts to set it down in front of her but snatches it back as he realizes what she has said. He holds the sandwich protectively against his chest.

Jack: Wait a darn minute, lady! You said there was a fire. What's going on here? You better get your story straight! *(Bea reaches for the sandwich, but Jack holds it away, out of reach.)*

Bea: Oh dear, it looks so good . . . .

Anna: Give her the sandwich. It's all right, Mr. Moore.

Jack reluctantly puts the plate down but remains standing above Bea, arms folded, glaring down at her.

Bea: *(takes a bite)* Too much mayo, but good. *(sips her tea)*

Anna: *(watches Bea chew for a minute then asks kindly)* Why did you lie to us?

Bea: *(takes another bite)* Well, I don't know you . . . .

Anna: I told you my name.

Bea: *(chewing)* I forgot.

Anna: Anna Kranze.

Bea: Oh yes. *(nods)* Now I remember. Anna. I like that. *(another bite)*

Anna: But you haven't told me your name.

Bea: No, I guess I haven't. *(nibbles coyly)*

Jack: *(harshly, acts like he may grab the sandwich back)* Quit beatin' around the bush! What's your name, lady? Spit it out.

Bea: *(whispers)* I'd rather not mention it just yet.

Anna: *(upset)* You mean to say, you won't tell me your name?

Bea: *(whispers)* Not right now. Maybe later.

Anna: *(very offended)* Well! For heaven's sake! After I bought you a nice egg salad sandwich and invited you to come home with me! *(Anna turns to Jack)* Did you ever hear of such a thing? *(Anna tucks her purse under her arm and starts to get up)* Maybe I did make a mistake. Maybe she is a criminal!

Bea: *(drops the sandwich, clutches Anna's arm)* Oh, no. Please. Wait! I wasn't thinking. Of course I'll tell you my name. Please don't go. You're the only friend I have in the world. *(begins to cry)* Don't go!

Anna: *(sits back down, totally confused)* Only friend? but I don't even know your name!

Bea: Beatrice Haverhill. Bea. Call me Bea.

Jack: *(extends his hand)* Pleased ta meetcha. I'm Jack Moore.

Bea: *(to Anna)* I'm afraid I forgot your name again.

Anna: *(very firmly)* Anna. Anna Kranze. Would it help if I wrote it down? *(fumbles in her purse for something to write with, locates a pencil and writes on a paper napkin during the following)*

Bea: It might.

Jack: If you forget mine, just look at the menu. *(points)* Jack's Diner.

Bea: Good. I don't know where my mind is these days. It's the medication. It makes me all fuzzy. I almost didn't remember where I hid my money, either.

Anna: *(slides the paper napkin across to Bea)* Here. Now you can remember. Anna Kranze. Just like it's spelled. See?

Bea: You're so kind. Anna. *(looks dangerously close to tears again)*

Jack: Ain't you gonna eat your nice sammich?

Bea: Oh, yes. *(nibbles at it some more, looking at Anna)* If I remember your name, can I still go home with you?

Anna: *(at a loss)* Well, yes. At least for the time being. I guess. Until we can locate your family.

Bea: *(drops the sandwich and clutches Anna's arm, very upset)* Oh no. We mustn't do that. Oh, no! No!

Anna: You don't want me to call your son?

Bea: Step-son. No please. Don't call him. Please don't.

Anna: I meant your own son.

Bea: *(confused)* What son? I don't have a son. Where did you get that idea?

Anna: But I thought . . . well, you said that your own son would be nice to you . . . .

Bea: *(finally gets it straight)* Oh, well, I meant to say that if I had a son, he would be a lot nicer to me.

Jack: I thought you had a son, too.

Bea: *(shakes her head)* No. Absolutely no son. You don't think a son of mine would let people treat his poor mother like this, do you?

Anna: Oh dear, I guess not . . . but you still need someone to take care of you.

Bea: No, I don't. I just need to get somewhere where I can cash a check. I can take perfectly good care of myself. I have absolutely no intention of going back there . . . . not on a platter!

Anna: But – –

Bea: You don't understand what they're trying to do to me.

Jack: What'd you mean?

Bea: *(conspiratorial)* They want to put me away – – so they can have it all. They're tired of waiting.

Anna: *(shocked)* What?

Bea: *(dramatic)* Yes! It's terrible, but it's true. Sonny never liked me.

Anna: That's awful!

Bea: Oh, yes. Awful.

Jack: *(He's really not convinced)* You mean . . . like somebody's trying to . . . to put you away, like a crazy person?

Bea: That's exactly right. I know another woman, Margaret Robbins. Her children had her committed to Sunnybrook so they could get their hands on her money. She's as sane as anyone, but they committed her just the same. And I always thought her children liked her!

Anna: *(shakes her head)* All this is really hard to believe. I never had children but it seems to me . . .

Bea: Oh, well – – there you are! You never had children! How can you know?

Anna: *(shocked)* But children are supposed to love their parents!

Bea: Supposed to . . . sure. But that's not always the case. *(takes a bite)* Some children will do anything to their parents . . .

Jack: Say! You tryin' to tell us your own kids burned down your house?

Anna: *(patiently)* No, Mr. Moore.

Jack: Boy, this really beats me! What kinda world are we livin' in when kids burn down their own mama's house? Boy! That's just awful!

Bea: They didn't burn my house.

Jack: *(puzzled)* No? Are you sure?

Bea: They just want to put me in a sanitarium! For crazy people!

Anna: A sanitarium!

Bea: And naturally, I don't want to go. I want to stay in my own home . . . but I can't.

Jack: Because it burned?

Bea: *(annoyed)* It didn't burn! Pay attention.

Jack: *(very confused)* But you said . . . .

Anna: *(very firmly)* It was a misunderstanding, Mr. Moore. There never was a fire. no fire!

Jack: Oh. *(finally gets it)* Oh! A misunderstanding. Right. I remember now. Sorry. I think I got a little lost.

Anna: Now go on, Bea. They want to put you in a sanitarium . . . .

Bea: Yes. And like I said, I don't want to go. There are sick people in there. I don't like to be around sick people. *(Twirls a finger at her temple, suggestively)*

Anna: *(at a loss)* Oh. Of course not.

Jack: *(feels like someone should say something)* Well, then. Don't go.

Bea: It's not that simple. *(puts the sandwich down)*

Anna: Go on.

Bea: They are very clever.

Anna: I guess I still don't understand. It is just that they don't love you?

Bea: More than that. They hate me. At least Sonny does. Veronica just goes along with whatever Sonny wants. She's just normally mean. Sonny's crazy mean. He would do just about anything to me that he thought he could get away with.

Anna: But why? Why does he hate you?

Bea: *(hunches forward)* Do you watch the soaps?

Anna: Soaps?

Bea: You know – – the SOAPS.

Anna: Oh, yes. Some of them.

Bea: It's a lot like on "Another Day." When Vixen stole Cinnamon's husband and he got a divorce so he could marry her. Cinnamon's child, Jonathon never forgave Vixen and the minute he got the chance, he took over her whole microchip corporation.

Anna: *(excited)* I remember! He staged a proxy fight and got control!

Jack: Huh? *(looks from one to the other of the women, totally lost again)*

Bea: That's just what happened to me! Only it all started forty years ago.

Jack: *(struggling to catch up)* That's a long time to carry a grudge. *(slides onto the bench besides Anna, in order to follow the conversation better)* Forty years!

Bea: Sonny was just biding his time!

Anna: Are you in the microchip business?

Bea: Well, no, that's one place where this is different.

Jack: I still don't understand. Why does . . . what's his name, Sonny . . . hate you so much?

Anna: *(making a brilliant assumption)* I think I know. *(points dramatically at Bea)* You must have been Vixen!

Bea: *(proud but modest)* Yes! I was the "other woman".

Jack: *(terribly shocked)* No!

Bea: Yes! I stole Sonny's father away from his mother. . . and he never forgave me . . . not for forty years!

Jack: Oh my! This is a fine kettle of fish!

Bea: *(carried away by the memories)* I just couldn't help myself. I fell madly in love. He was so handsome. He swept me off my feet. He never loved Sonny's mother anyway. She deliberately got herself pregnant so he would have to marry her. *(confidently)* Of course, that was before he met me.

Anna: *(totally caught up in the story)* Just like on "The Coming Storm".

Bea: *(thumps the table, making Jack and Anna jump)* Exactly! She trapped him!

Jack: The little schemer!

Bea: Then, when Sonny was only three, his Daddy and I fell in love. We couldn't help ourselves. It was a veritable storm of passion.

Jack: *(marveling)* Gee.

Bea: *(dramatically)* She always tried to make trouble for us. She turned Sonny against me and he never got over it. It was the only flaw in our perfect lives.

Jack: It's just like a soap opera!

Bea: That's what I'm trying to tell you. I helped my husband build up his business into a big success and he made a lot of money. And now that he's dead and I'm all alone, Sonny sees his chance to get even!

Anna: By putting you in a sanitarium?

Bea: *(nods)* And telling everyone I'm crazy and taking all my money.

Jack: Gee!

Anna: What are you going to do?

Bea: *(proudly)* I already did it! I ran away! I took everything I could carry and called a cab. I'm going to get a check cashed and find a safe place to stay and – –

Anna: But you've already got a place to stay. With me, remember?

Bea: What did you say your name was?

Anna: *(taps the napkin)* Anna Kranze!

Bea: Of course. I remember. Anna.

Anna: Right!

Bea: *(jumps up)* Good. Well, now you know the whole story so let's get going!

Jack: *(offended)* Hey, you didn't finish your nice sammich!

Bea: Oh. Yeah. Sorry. *(stuffs the remainder in her pocket without bothering to wrap it)* I'll take it with me and eat it later. Let's get going. I might have been followed. Do you live far?

Anna: *(floundering)* Oh, uh, no, not far. I have to pay for your sandwich. Just a minute. How much is it, Mr. Moore?

Jack: Two bucks. *(Anna pulls two bills out of her purse and hands them to Jack.)*

Jack: *(takes the money)* Thanks.

Bea: *(stops abruptly and glares at Anna)* Just a minute! Haven't you forgotten something?

Anna: What?

Bea: *(scolding)* You forgot the TIP!

Anna: *(meekly)* Oh. Yes, I guess I did. *(gives Bea a look as if she is wondering what she has gotten herself into, then digs into her purse and puts some change down on the table)*

Jack: *(raises his eyebrows and shrugs slightly, smiling, pockets the coins)* Thanks.

Bea: Now, let's hurry! *(tugs Anna toward the door)*

Anna: Wait! You're forgetting your things!

Bea: *(stops)* Oh yes. My things. *(gathers up the two pillow cases and the shopping bag, lifts them sadly)* I couldn't bring much.

Jack: *(sees an opening to satisfy his curiosity)* Say, what did you grab, anyway? I always wondered what I'd save if there was a fire.

Bea: *(exasperated)* I wish you'd pay attention! There wasn't any fire!

Jack: *(indignant)* I know that! I just meant what would I save if there was a fire? How did you decide what to take with you?

Bea: Well, I had to think fast while Veronica was at a Guild meeting . . . And I wasted a lot of time looking for my shoes.

Jack: *(points at her slippers)* I noticed you didn't find 'em.

Bea: She hides them so I can't go out.

Anna: You were practically a prisoner.

Bea: *(grim)* I was a prisoner! She hid my shoes so I couldn't go out and never gave me any money. I saved every cent I could get my hands on for my get-away.

Jack: Didn't you try to tell someone . . . your friends – – somebody?

Bea: I tried, but Veronica told them all that I was having mental problems. Nobody would believe me. Then she took my phone out. I had to use the phone in Sonny's study where they could listen in. It was like a jail. And then the medication always made me so fuzzy. I couldn't remember anybody's number.

Jack: That's the most awful thing I ever heard.

Anna: *(horrified)* We can't let them get away with this.

Bea: I finally figured out that the medication was in my banana custard. I thought it was funny that Veronica would go to the trouble to make me custard every day. One day I spilled it all but I didn't tell her because I didn't want her to get mad at me, but that day I wasn't so fuzzy so I figured it out. I hated to give up my custard, but I just hate that fuzzy feeling more.

Jack: *(pokes one of the bundles)* I'm still curious about what you took with you . .

Bea: *(opens the pillow case and pulls out a few things as she talks)* Well, I took my clothes, some of them . . . and my sun hat . . . and my jewelry . . . . I sure don't want her to get her hands on that.

Jack: I should say not.

Bea: And my medicine – – the good pills, for my arthritis, not the fuzzy stuff. And I took all my pictures of my husband, but I left all the ones of Sonny – – even the ones on the pony.

Jack: I don't blame you for that!

Bea: And I took my measuring spoons, and my husband's silver hairbrushes I gave him . . . and my hot curlers and my water pik.

Jack: *(being helpful)* And your toaster . . . .

Bea: *(sharply)* How did you know that? I didn't say anything about a toaster!

Jack: *(stricken, realizes he's trapped himself, tries to recover)* I, uh, I just guessed. It, uh . . . seemed logical. A toaster comes in handy . . .

Bea: You didn't snoop in my stuff, did you!

Jack: *(holds up hands in shocked innocence)* God forbid!

Bea: Well, you're a good guesser. I did take a toaster, but it wasn't mine. She ruined mine. Stuck a fork in it trying to pry an English muffin loose. Too bad that it didn't finish her off, but it had a wooden handle. But it ruined my pretty toaster. *(pulls a toaster out of one of the bags)* So I took hers!

Jack: Nice.

Anna: Very nice.

Bea: Well, it's not as good as the one she broke.

Anna: But, that seems a little heavy to take on a getaway. Couldn't you have just bought a new one – – after you got your check cashed?

Bea: *(returns the toaster to the bag)* It was the principal of the thing. I wanted this toaster!

Jack: I can understand that!

Bea: *(adamant)* She owed it to me.

Anna: *(not quite sure what to say)* I s-see. Well, it's okay with me.

Jack: *(heartily)* Sure. me. too!

Bea: *(satisfied)* Good. Well, let's go. *(gathers up her stuff)* We're not getting any younger.

Jack: *(whispers to Anna)* I hope you know what you're getting into, Miz Kranze.

Anna: *(whispers back)* Me, too.

Bea: Things are certainly getting interesting, aren't they? At least we're doing something! This sure beats being fuzzy all the time.

Anna: *(rather pleasently surprised at the thought)* Well, yes! I guess you can definitely say that things are getting interesting!

Bea: Let's get going!

END OF THE FIRST ACT.

ACT TWO, SCENE ONE

About four weeks later. At rise: The diner is about the same as before, except there are Thanksgiving decorations, instead of Halloween. The clock on the wall says 3:05.
Anna and Virginia are seated with tea paraphanalia at their usual table. Virginia is wearing a warmer coat than in the previous scene. Anna looks much different than before. Her hair is much prettier and she is wearing a stylish, well made new outfit. Her general appearance is younger and more attractive and she is illuminated with a new vivacity. Jack is working around the place as they chat.

Virginia: I can't believe it's going so well, are you sure there isn't something you're not telling me?

Anna: *(animated)* Not a thing. I'm really having fun. After we got her new shoes, she had to have clothes and new sunglasses. She loves to wear sunglasses. It took days to find everything. She likes the colors to match up. We had to go to all sorts of cute stores to find the right pink. She LOVES to shop. You know, I've never even been in some of those stores before. Every Friday we go shopping at the fancy new market over on Beech street. She won't eat fish, but we both like chicken. They have real fresh chicken over there. And good Kosher pickles.

Virginia: Beech Street? That gourmet place?

Anna: That's the one, by the park. Bea found it. On Saturdays, we go into the city for a matinee. Last week it was a musical. That's probably why I wasn't home when you tried to call.

Virginia: A matinee?

Anna: Right. Bea has *(not her own words)* "always had an af-inity for", you know, *(airily)* "the the-ah-ter". On Sundays, we just ramble around, here and there. Walking is good for her arthritis. We look at pictures.

Virginia: Moving pictures?

Anna: No, paintings. You know. At the galleries. *(proudly)* I'm thinking about taking watercolor classes.

Virginia: *(jealous, but trying to hide it)* Really?

Anna: Well, like Bea says, we've got better fish to fry than to sit home and watch our toenails grow. *(laughs gaily)* I just never realized how many fun things there are to do in the city!

Virginia: *(a little flat)* Isn't that nice. *(She sips her tea thoughtfully, looking at Anna over the rim. Oblivious to Virginia's mood, Anna digs in her purse and pulls out a little pink paper packet which she empties into her cup, stirs and sips.)* What's that?

Anna: Saccharin. I'm on a diet.

Virginia: A diet? Since when?

Anna: *(laughs)* Oh, that Bea! She made me join an exercise class. Says I'm too hippy. She bet me a new dress that I couldn't lose ten pounds by Christmas.

Virginia: I thought you looked a little . . . different . . .

Anna: Well, I've only lost about three pounds, but I'm working on it. I met some lovely new women over at the Health Club. Widows, too.

Virginia: You're getting awfully involved with her . . . *(sips her tea)* I mean, what if her step-son tries to make trouble? He might even sue you.

Anna: How? We've gone all over that. I didn't even know Bea until after she ran away. She's just my boarder.

Virginia: Well, I guess . . .

Jack: *(carries two plates of cake to the table)* Here you go, ladies, some very special carrot cake. *(looks around)* Say, where's Bea? I thought she was gonna come, too.

Anna: Still at the beauty shop, remember? Today's Wednesday. *(to Virginia)* She gets her nails done on Wednesday.

Virginia: *(eyeing the cake)* That looks delicious! *(cuts off a bite, tastes)* Ummm. It is! I'll bet it's got a million calories.

Jack: *(to Anna)* I just gave you a little piece to try, Miz Kranze, because of your diet.

Anna: That's plenty big enough.

Virginia: Is this a new recipe, Mr. Moore? It's marvelous!

Jack: Well, yeah, sorta. Bea had me take my regular recipe and double the butter then add a half a cup of sour cream and half a cup of nuts. I think it really helps. That Bea's fulla good ideas. *(Virginia reacts.)*

Anna: *(tasting)* She was sure right about the nuts.

Jack: She made me use real vanilla, too, instead of that cheap stuff I always usta use.

Virginia: *(rather hates to admit it)* Well, it is delicious.

Jack: That Bea. Ain't she somethin? I never saw anybody on the go so much, for a lady her age. Don't she about wear you out, Miz Kranze?

Anna: *(laughs)* I'll say! This is wonderful!

Jack: *(modestly)* Thanks.

Virginia: Well, I must say, all this running around does seem to be agreeing with you. I haven't seen you look so . . . so lively in years.

Anna: *(eating)* It's awfully sweet of you to come over here for lunch today. I know how busy you are.

Virginia: I just wanted to see for myself.

Anna: *(smiles, beginning to tune in with greater sensitivity to Virginia's feeling)* I told you it was working out . . .

Virginia: *(looking for something wrong)* Yes, well, I suppose she's coming up with the rent and all, like she agreed?

Anna: *(nods, smiling)* $100 a week. Only four and a half weeks so far, but it sure helps. Of course she pays for lots of other stuff . . . like taxis and the theatre tickets. She just insists . . . says she likes to.

Jack: *(whistles)* Maybe I outta get a border.

Virginia: It's not like you need the money . . .

Anna: *(pats Virginia's hand)* Oh, yes, I do, dear. David didn't leave me as much as you think. Most of it is in very slow stocks. It hasn't been easy.

Virginia: *(surprised)* I didn't know that!

Anna: I've had to be very careful.

Virginia: You never said a word!

Anna: For a while I thought I'd have to give up the apartment. I wanted to get a job . . . any kind of a job, but what could I do? And at my age? And with no experience . . .?

Jack: *(chatty)* It's tough to get a job without experience.

Anna: *(eating)* That's right, and I just couldn't get myself pulled together enough to try to do something about it.

Jack: Didja think about going back to school?

Roscoe enters from outside, glances rather carefully at the two women, then waits beside the cash register. Jack breaks away and goes to wait on him. Roscoe buys a pack of cigarettes, still looking at the two women. They eat their cake, etc., paying him only slight interest. Jack rings up the sale, through the following:

Anna: *(to Virginia)* You know, I did think about going back to school. I always used to be very interested in math.

Virginia: You were? I never know that?

Anna: It was a long time ago . . . I'd have to catch up on the new computers . .

Virginia: *(stares at her)* It's almost like you were changing into a whole different person or something. *(a little hurt)* I feel like I hardly know you . . .

Anna: Oh no, don't feel that way. I just never wanted you to know about the money thing. You would worry.

Virginia: But the math. I never knew about that, either.

Anna: Oh – – it just never came up, that's all.

Virginia: Still . . .

> *Behind them, as they continue the following, Roscoe shows Jack a small square of paper. Jack squints at it, puts on his glasses, looks again, reacts briefly and then make his face expressionless.*

Anna: *(smiling)* Don't worry about it.

Virginia: *(lowers her eyes, ashamed of her feelings)* I'm being silly, aren't I?

Anna: *(very kind)* It's all right. I understand. *(She pats Virginia's hand. Embarrassed by all these unfamiliar feelings, they attend to their food, smiling shyly at each other across the table, feeling very close.)*

Jack: *(to Roscoe)* Nope. Never saw her. Sorry.

Roscoe: Thanks. *(replaces the photo in his pocket and exits)*

Jack: *(rushes back to the women, very upset)* Did you see that guy? The one who was just in here? He had a pitcher of Bea!

Anna: *(alarmed)* What?

Jack: Bea. He had a little pitcher of Bea. Wanted to know if I knew who it was.

Anna: Oh dear.

Jack: Yeah! I bet he was a detective! That's the way they operate when they're lookin' for someone . . . take a pitcher around and ask everybody if they know who it is.

Anna: A detective! Oh, no! *(wringing her hands)* How did he know to come here?

Jack: I dunno . . . maybe the cab driver remembered her or something . . . when she first come here. She did look kinda crazy that day. He might've remembered.

Anna: Especially when she took her money out of her house shoe!

Virginia: Her what?

Anna: Her house shoe. She used to hide every penny she could find in the toe of those red house slippers. Remember, she came in here with just one shoe on?

Virginia: Oh, I remember.

Jack: If I was a cab driver and some goofy old woman paid me out of a shoe, I'd remember.

25

Anna: That must be it.

Virginia: *(uneasy)* Well, what are we going to do?

Anna: *(hops up)* I'd better get right over to the beauty shop and tell her to go straight home.

Jack: Good idea. Tell her to keep outta sight. *(runs behind the counter)* Just a minute. I got something for her. *(stuff something into a small paper bag and hand it to Anna)* Here.

Anna: What is it?

Jack: Her piece of carrot cake. Just in case she don't get back in here for a little while. My treat.

Anna: That's very nice, Mr. Moore. She'll appreciate that.

Jack: Hey! Bea's special.

Virginia: *(to Anna)* Do you want me to go with you? *(wants to go)*

Anna: Oh no. It's just down the block. *(pauses, realizing that Virginia's feeling left out of the drama)* Well, unless you want to go . . .

Virginia: *(feeling a little rejected)* Well, I do have time.

Anna: Sure . . . come on then! Hurry.

Virginia: *(snatching up her things)* If you're sure I won't be in the way . . . *(wild horses couldn't keep her away)*

Anna: Don't be silly. Come on. *(pauses at the register.)* My treat for lunch today. *(to Jack)* How much?

Jack: Three bucks.

Anna proudly hands him three one dollar bills, starts to put her money away then remembers and quickly adds (with a little flourish) another fifty cents. Jack and Virginia look at each other with amusement at what Anna has done, and thinking of Bea's tipping obsession, they smile.

Jack and Virginia: *(together)* For the tip!

Jack: *(shakes his fondly)* You ladies are somethin' else!

Anna and Virginia run out. After a moment, the door opens and the detective, Roscoe, enters casually, from the direction opposite that of the women. He hitches his pants and glances around the empty diner. Jack looks up, starts slightly as he recognizes him.

Jack: *(trying to be casual)* Oh, back again, huh?

Roscoe: Yeah. Decided I might's well take a break and get a cuppa coffee as long as I was here. *(hitches crudely at his pants, shambles over to the other bench and sits, his back against the outside wall of the diner, so that he faces in. He props up his feet on the opposite bench and loosens his belt, making himself more comfortable. Jack looks undecided for a minute then picks up the coffee pot and a mug.)*

Roscoe: Man, oh man. I gotta get a different line a work.

Jack: *(studying Roscoe, eyes narrowed)* That's what I always say, too. Being on your feet all day is murder. Coffee?

Roscoe: Yeah. Oh well, things are lookin' pretty good. At least I got one good lead.

Jack: *(tries to remain casual, despite his alarm, pours the coffee, spilling a little)* Oh, yeah? *(wipes it up with his apron)*

Roscoe: Yeah. Lady at that fancy dan supermarket over on Beech remembers seeing my old dame.

Jack: *(frowning)* Oh, yeah?

Roscoe: Yeah. Says she's been in several times. Always gets one big pickle is how she remembers her. Funny what sticks in a person's mind. *(chuckles)* Pickles!

Jack: Well, I never seen her in here. But, uh, all old ladies looks alike to me.

Roscoe: *(confidentially)* I didn't say nothin' before, but I figure you for a savvy guy. I'm a detective, see. *(points a finger at Jack like a gun, and winks, knowingly)* Had me pegged, didn't you? *(Jack nods, very uncomfortable. Roscoe nods, pleased with himself)* I thought so. I can always tell a savvy guy. *(hands Jack a business card)* Hang onto that, Mac, in case you ever need a good confidential snoop job.

Jack: *(with distaste)* Yeah, sure. Thanks. *(sticks the card in his pocket)* Uh, say, what'dya think will happen to the, uh, old broad . . . uh, after you turn her in?

Roscoe: *(shrugs)* How do I know? *(looks around)* Say, you make decent pie?

Jack: *(mechanically)* Apple, cherry, chocolate cream.

Roscoe: Why not, as long as I'm takin' a break? Gimme . . . uh, chocolate. *(pulls a racing form out of his pocket and starts to read)*

Jack is momentarily at a loss, cannot think of a way to get Roscoe back on the subject. Frustrated, he decides to continue "business as usual" and retreats toward the counter.

The door opens and Bea enters. Her whole appearance is vastly different. She moves with assurance and brisk steps. She is wearing fancy sunglasses and a stiff, elaborate red wig and a color-matched, bright polyester pants suit outfit and flashy jewelry, including big dangly earrings. She closes the door, pats her hair with a deliberate gesture and then walks to her usual place and sits down, facing Roscoe. Jack does not recognize her.

Jack: Be right with you, ma'm. *(He carries the piece of pie right past Bea's table and puts it down in front of Roscoe, who begins to eat, oblivious to Bea. Jack then walks back to Bea, still not recognizing her and offers her a menu.)* Here you go. Want a little time to look it over?

Bea: *(unaware that he doesn't recognize her)* Hi. No. I'm just waiting for Anna. *(She removes her sunglasses. Jack does a horrified double-take as he recognizes Bea. He quickly moves so that his back is more to Roscoe, and begins to try to* *warn her, with body English, that this man is a danger to her. Bea just doesn't comprehend. Her mind is entirely on her new appearance. She pats her unbelievable hairdo with self-conscious pride.)* Well, aren't you going to say anything? *(Jack pantomimes wildly. Roscoe, still reading, is unaware of any of this.)* I always wanted to be a redhead. Does it look too wiggy? *(Jack continues to try to warn her, and Bea finally becomes aware of his antics, laughs.)* For heaven's sake, what on earth's the matter?

Roscoe: *(calls out without really looking up)* How about a warm-up, Mac? *(holds out his mug)*

Jack: *(rolls his eyes, helpless)* Sure thing. Coming right up. *(Jack gives up, throws his hands in the air and heads for the coffeepot. Bea looks curiously after him for a minute, shrugs and pulls out her pocket mirror to examine her hair. She primps while Jack nervously refills the detective's mug, then he rushes back to Bea. He leans over her shoulder, pretending to polish the table with his apron, and whispers desperately to Bea)* That guy's a private detective. He's looking for you. Get outta here!

Bea: What's that, Mr. Moore? Speak up. You know I'm a little deaf.

Jack: *(at a loss)* That guy . . . Uh, Ummm. . . Uh, uh. .

Bea: What?

Virginia: *(rushes in, not noticing Roscoe)* Oh, for heaven's sake. You're right, it IS her!

Anna: *(at Virginia's heels)* We've been looking all over for you. You won't believe it! Did you tell her yet, Mr. Moore?

Jack pantomimes to them that the detective has returned. Roscoe continues to read his paper, ignoring the others. Anna recognizes the man and reacts, with great alarm. She clutches Virginia's arm.

Anna: *(whispers)* Good Lord! It's him! What'll we do?

Virginia: *(thru clenched teeth)* Act natural. Maybe he doesn't know.

Anna: *(To Bea, trying to act natural, but not doing too well)* So! Here you are . . . *(desperately)* Uh, Agatha!

Virginia: *(meaningfully)* Yes, uh, Agatha . . . we finally found you.

Bea: *(very puzzled)* What? *(Virginia and Anna slide onto the benches at Bea's table, Anna next to Bea, Virginia across, her back to the detective.)*

Anna: *(whispers)* That man is looking for you. We think he's a detective.

Jack: *(whispers)* He is! He told me! *(Anna and Virginia react with greater alarm)*

Bea: What? I must have soap in my ears. I can't understand anybody today. Speak up, Anna.

Anna: *(tries again, whispering)* Don't look now. See that man over there? *(Bea tries to look at the man, but Anna stops her.)* Don't look now!

Bea: What is going on here? Everyone's crazy today!

Roscoe: *(stands up, digs in his pocket for some money and heads for the cash register, counts out his change and speaks to Jack, who scuttles over to block Roscoe's view of Bea)* Well, back to work. What'd I owe you? *(Bea struggles to get a look at the man, but her friends keep getting in the way so he can't see her.*

Jack: *(directs Roscoe's turn away from Bea, rather like a bullfighter, leading a bull)* Right over here, uh, Mac. Uh, oh, uh, yeah, a buck eighty-five.

Roscoe: Here you go.

Jack: Thanks.

Bea is still trying to get a look at him, and the others are whispering desperately to her. Roscoe starts to leave the diner, then turns back and heads toward the ladies' table. Anna clutches Bea's arm, protectively. They fall silent as he approaches, watching him.

Roscoe: Excuse me, ladies. I wonder if you could help me out. I'm trying to find my, er, great aunt Beatrice Haverhill. *(Bea does a double-take, but Roscoe doesn't notice.)* She's staying with some, er, friends in this neighborhood, but I've lost the address and I wanted to go by and say hello. I wonder if you might know her? *(winks at Jack over their heads, as if to share his cleverness, hands Virginia the snapshot, then Anna and Virginia quickly shake their heads "no" but Bea grabs the picture. Anna and Virginia are too shocked by Bea's move to react.)*

Bea: Let's see that. *(studies the snapshot critically)* Your. . . "aunt", you say?

Roscoe: *(another knowing glance at Jack)* Dear, old, Great-Aunt Beatrice. I haven't seen her in years.

Bea: *(with emphasis)* Well, what a sweet-looking old lady. Just look at that pretty WHITE hair. I'd certainly remember her. *(pats her new red hair)* Nope, never saw her before. Sorry.

Roscoe: *(takes picture)* Oh well, thanks anyway. Have a nice day.

Bea: *(wickedly)* And . . . good luck in finding your – – great-aunt!

Roscoe: Thanks. *(The friends watch as Roscoe leaves the diner. Bea pulls a small mirror out of her purse and primps.)*

Anna: *(pounces)* Oh, Bea! How could you?

Bea: *(misunderstands)* Well, I hoped you'd like it. I always wanted to be a red-head. *(consults mirror)* It's just a wig. I thought if I really like it, I could have my own dyed later, if it's not too darn thin. What do you think?

Anna: I don't mean your hair! I mean that man!

Virginia: He's a detective. He told Mr. Moore he's looking for you.

Bea: *(examining her face in mirror)* I always hated that picture. Sonny took it at the lake. It makes me look so old.

Anna: Bea, this is serious! They know where you are!

Jack: Yeah!

Bea: No, they don't. Not yet, or he wouldn't be showing that awful picture around.

Jack: Hey, that's right!

Virginia: I don't understand . . . are you just going to sit there?

Anna: Why didn't you wait for me at the beauty shop, like you said you would?

Bea: *(lowers mirror)* Oh, Anna dear, don't scold me. I wanted to surprise you. Do you like it? *(To Virginia)*

Virginia: *(trying to be tactful)* It sure takes the years off. What an, uh, interesting color.

Anna: Oh, for heaven's sake! Stop worrying about her hair! This is terrible! What are we going to do?

Bea: *(puts mirror away)* I think we should go to Hawaii.

Jack: huh?

Anna: What?

Jack: Where?

Virginia: Hawaii?

Bea: Why not? I saw a magazine about it at the beauty shop. It looked so nice and warm. I've always wanted to go. This is as good a time as any.

Jack: Maybe better.

Anna: Oh dear, I don't think I could afford . . .

Bea: Oh, I'll take care of the tickets . . . and everything. My treat.

Jack: Jeeze, you'd think it was a piece of carrot cake! Hawaii. Jeeze!

Virginia: You know, I think Bea's right. Get out of town.

Bea: Right. As quick as we can. *(stands up)* But first I gotta go to the ladies room. *(exits to the ladies room)*

Virginia: Gosh. *(wistful)* Hawaii. Imagine! Harry always said we'd go one day, but we never did.

Jack: I always wanted to see them palm trees . . . just like Miami Beach.

Anna: It's going to cost a lot . . .

Virginia: She said it would be her treat.

Anna: Oh, dear I don't know if I should.

Jack: Man-oh-man, I wish somebody would invite me to Hawaii!

Anna: There's so much to think about.

Virginia: You'd better start a list.

Anna: Oh, gosh. *(taking a paper napkin, digs pencil out of purse, starts to write)* Let's see. Go to the cleaners. *(writes)* Get Bea's prescription refilled. *(writes)* We can't leave without that. And . . .

Virginia: *(interrupts)* Is Bea sick?

Anna: I don't think so. Don't mention it to her – she hates to talk about anything to do with sick people. It's just some little white pills. She takes four a day. It's probably for her arthritis.

Virginia: Oh, well. Get it refilled twice and take it with you.

Anna: I haven't been anywhere in years. Should I stop the mail?

Jack: Sure.

Anna: I don't even know if I can find my suitcase.

Jack: This is gonna do you a lotta good!

Anna: *(Getting excited)* I suppose it will.

Bea: *(returns from the restroom)* Don't let me forget to pick up my perscription, Anna, I'm almost out. I'll need to take it with me. You'd better start us a list of things to get ready.

Anna: I already have. *(holds up napkin)*

Bea: Good. Put down, "Take your books back to the library."

Anna: *(writing)* And get our tickets.

Bea: I'll have to be sure to pack some long-sleeved shirts. I'm sort of, uh, allergic, to the sun, but I love it anyway.

Anna: *(hesitant)* Uh, how long will we be gone, do you think?

Bea: How long? Well, who knows? Until we get bored, I guess. How does that sound? Now where did I put my sun hat?

Anna: Oh, I'm really so excited! I wonder where I put the camera? I haven't used it since David took me to the Poconos. How long ago was that? I can't remember!

Virginia: Is there anything I can do to help?

Anna: Do we need a passport for Hawaii?

Jack: Ain't it a state?

Anna: *(laughs)* Oh, of course. I forgot. Silly me.

Virginia: What about traveler's checks?

Bea: I'll call the bank. They'll take care of it for us.

Anna: I'll put it on the list, anyway.

> *The door opens and Roscoe re-enters. The women lose their joy and grow instantly stiff with apprehension. They look at each other, alarmed, wondering what he is doing back so soon. Jack moves uncertainly toward the detective, half wanting to stay near Bea to protect her.*

Roscoe: *(cheery)* Here I am again, like a bad penny.

Jack: Yeah. Hi.

Roscoe: *(holds up a bill)* Just need some change for the pay phone on the corner. Can you break this for me?

Jack: *(anything to get rid of him)* Sure. *(He gestures to the women to be quiet, goes to the register, makes change. Roscoe pays absolutely no attention to the women.)*

Roscoe: Looks like I just about, ush, got those *(winks)* uh, details all wrapped up . . . you know, what we was talking about earlier. I found out where the old broad's staying, so it's just a matter of time.

Jack: *(stunned)* Yeah? Oh yeah! I remember.

Roscoe: Gotta call my office. Thanks for the change. See you around. *(exits)*

Jack: Sure. *(rushes back to the women)* Oh golly, the fat's in the fire now. He's onto you, for sure, Bea. You gotta get outta town quick, he knows where you live!

Anna: *(very nervous)* Oh, Bea, we've got to hurry. *(jumps up)*

Virginia: Don't waste a second!

Bea is strangely still, like someone listening to a far-distant sound. Anna and Virginia scramble into their coats, but Bea moves much more slowly.

Virginia: You've got to get packed. I've got a new tote bag you can borrow, if you need it, Anna.

Anna: How sweet. Yes, I can probably use it.

Virginia: It's bright red.

Anna: Oh, good.

Jack: Lemme give you some sugars to take with you . . . for your coffee and stuff, I don't think they like fake sugar in Hawaii. *(giver her a handful of little packets)* Here.

Anna: *(dazed by the speed of events)* Oh, thanks. *(drops them in her purse)*

Virginia: This is so exciting! Just like a soap!

Jack: You better get goin'.

Virginia: I'll come home with you. If that man tries to follow or anything, I'll do something to throw him off.

Jack: Good idea. *(The women hurry toward the door, Bea a few steps behind the others. Jack notices that Bea has left her little paper sack of carrot cake behind. He grabs it and runs after them.)* Wait! You forgot your carrot cake.

Bea turns back to take the little present from Jack. She takes it, and on an impulse, takes his hand, leans up and kisses Jack on the cheek. She become very still, almost suspended in motion, looking at him . . .

Bea: Thank you, Jack. I won't ever forget you. You've been a good friend.

Jack: *(a little embarrassed)* Well, heck, it's just a piece of cake. And anyway, it was your idea, the nuts and all. *(gives her an awkward little pat)* You take care of yourself, Bea. Hear me? If that jerk comes back in here lookin' for you, I'll throw him off the track. I'll tell him you went to Canada or somethin'.

Anna: For heaven's sake, Bea, come on! *(She finally senses that Bea is in some sort of strange mood, hesitates.)* Bea? *(Anna gives the others a worried look.)* Aren't you coming?

Virginia: *(to Bea)* Come on!

Anna: Bea? What's wrong, dear?

Bea: Anna, come back and sit down for a minute.

Anna: What? Sit down? Why? What are you talking about, Bea? We got to get home and start packing. *(gestures toward the door)* That man. That detective. We gotta go!

Bea: *(sits, points to opposite bench)* Just for a minute.

Anna: *(sits, mystified and frustrated. The others watch in silence, wondering.)* What is it, Bea?

Bea: Do you remember the Promise you told me about . . . the one you made with Virginia?

Anna: *(laughs, a little embarrassed)* Yes, but wha. . . .?

Bea: *(interrupts)* I want to do that.

Anna: Do what?

Bea: Make a promise, like you did with Virginia. Only, this time, you and me. *(Virginia starts to speak, but Jack touches her arm and silences her.)*

Anna: *(looks to the others for support then turns uncertainly back to Bea, laughing nervously)* Oh, that was just a child's game. It didn't mean anything. *(a little frightened)*

Bea: I know, but then, I'm just a childish old woman. It won't take long. Humor me.

Anna: Well, all right, if we hurry, but it's just a game. We used to do it when we were girls. . . .

Bea: I know, in Brooklyn. Show me what to do.

Anna: Okay. *(puts her elbows on table)* Well, you just link little fingers, like this. *(They do it.)* And then you just, uh . . . make a promise.

Bea: Can you promise anything?

Anna: *(embarrassed laugh)* I guess so, it's just. . .

Bea: *(interrupts)* Well, I want you to make me a promise, Anna.

Anna: Oh. *(shrugs)* Well, sure. What do you want me to promise. To pay you back for the trip to Hawaii? *(giggles nervously)* I hope not!

Bea: Not that. I just want you to promise me that no matter what happens. . . even if we never get to Hawaii . . . that you won't go back into your shell. That you'll keep on having fun . . . like the last few weeks.

Anna: *(confused and a little upset)* Well, sure if that's what you want. I promise, but it seems awfully silly.

Bea: *(still serious)* Is there any more?

Anna: No, that's all there is to it. Like I told you, it's just a silly game.

Bea: *(unhooks her finger)* I know it's just a game, *(with emphasis)* But it still counts.

Anna: Oh, well, sure, if you want it to. But Bea, dear, we've just got to get going before that man comes back!

Virginia: *(trying to laugh it off)* Honestly, Bea! schoolgirl promises when Sonny may be on his way to get you right now! Sometimes I think you're losing your marbles!

Bea: *(briskly and matter of fact)* You wouldn't say that if you didn't like me, Virginia. *(gets up)* Now, come on girls, we got a hell of a lotta things to do! Let's get going!

Virginia: Well, it's about time!

BLACKOUT

Act Two, Scene Two

Same Day, Evening. At Rise: the clock on the dinner wall reads 8:45. It is dark outside. Jack is alone. He seems restless and worried.

Anna: *(rushes in, very distraught)* Oh, my God! She's not here, either! Have you seen Bea? I can't find her anywhere!

Jack: *(concerned)* No! I ain't seen her since she left with you . . . four, five hours ago. I been kinda worried about her, too. I just tried to call your place. No one answered. What's wrong?

Anna: Oh, Mr. Moore, I just know something's happened to her! I went out to get my cleaning, you know, my blue coat?

Jack: Yeah.

Anna: I couldn't leave it at the cleaners all the time we were going to be in Hawaii . . . and when I came back, the apartment door was standing half-open and she wasn't there.

Jack: Ah, Jeeze, I was afraid of somethin' like this!

Anna: Some of her things are gone, too! I found her new wig on the floor. She never would have put it there!

Jack: Ah, Jeeze, no. That's bad!

Anna: Oh, Jack, I think Sonny came and got her!

Jack: You didn't find no note or nothin'?

Anna: I looked all around. I found this on the table by the door. *(shows him a small paper sack)* It's her prescription. They must have delivered it while I was out.

Jack: I had this feeling that something was wrong, in my bones, you know? I been worrying about Bea all evening. Damn!

Anna: What are we going to do?

Jack: I don't know. I never was involved in nothin' like this before. Kidnappin' his own step-mother! Who ever heard of such a thing?

Anna: *(paces frantically)* I never felt so helpless in my life! My best friend taken right out of my own house and I don't know what to do! I think I'm going to lose my mind!

Jack: Ah, Jeeze, don't do that, Miz Kranze, we ain't licked yet. *(They stare at each other, trying to think.)* You know, there's one thing we're forgettin' about.

Anna: *(grasping)* What?

Jack: Well, we can't just rule Bea out of this, you know.

Anna: What do you mean?

Jack: Well, she got away from them once before, didn't she? Now she knows she can come to you for help, so first chance she gets, she's gonna call you to come get her!

Anna: That's right! She will! *(crumbles)* But . . . if they give her that other medicine, she'll get all fuzzy and she won't remember the number.

Jack: *(frowns)* Jeeze!

Anna: *(crying)* She can't even remember my name when she takes that medicine. I'll never see her again!

Jack: Oh, now, don't give up! Sure you will. *(temporarily at a loss)* Damn! Listen, Miz Kranze . . . you gotta think positive. Like Bea always done. She outfoxed them once, didn't she? She'll do it again. She'll find a way to get out, no matter what they give her.

Anna: Do you really think so?

Jack: Sure! Hey, she'll make monkeys outta them guys, mark my words. You'll be laughing about it with her in Hawaii before you know it, you and Bea!

Anna: Do you think she'll try to come back here to the diner, or go home?

Jack: Gee, I dunno . . .

Anna: *(freshly alarmed)* Maybe she's trying to call right now, and there's no one home. I'd better get right back! *(starts for the door)*

Jack: I'll keep my eyes peeled in case she turns up here. I don't go home until ten.

Anna: Call me the minute you hear anything!

Jack: I will.

> *Anna exits. Jack scratches his head, looks around restlessly and begins to fiddle with the catsup bottles at the back, upset and distracted. After a beat, the door opens again and Roscoe enters from the opposite direction, a big grin on his face. He hitches at his pants and shambles across to lean chumily on the counter. Jack turns, sees him and slams down the bottle he was holding.*

Jack: You! What're you doin' back here?

Roscoe: *(not recognizing Jack's hostility, still grinning like a canary-eating cat)* Just winding up a few loose ends. Thought you might like to hear how it worked out . . . with the old broad . . .

Jack: *(recognizes the opportunity to pump him)* Right. Uh, say, *(looking after Anna)* How did it go? Did, did you find your, uh, "old broad"?

Roscoe: *(very chummy)* Does a cat find a mouse? Gimme a beer. I wanna unwind. These things always get me all worked up. *(cracks his knuckles)*

Jack: *(eyes narrowed, getting dangerous)* Tell me all about it.

Roscoe: *(bragging)* Well, like I told you, I already knew the general neighborhood where the old broad was hiding out. I was over at the drug store, trying to con the delivery kid outta the rest of the address . . . and while I was at it, picking up some rubbers. *(lowers his voice, very chummy)* There's this hot little number over at the dime store, see, and me and her's got a late date, after she gets off tonight. Ready Freddy, that's me . . . well, anyway, while I was hangin' around, waitin' on the kid, my old broad calls up and orders a double refill on something because . . . now get this, Mac . . . she's leaving town right away! Talk about your lucky breaks! Well, I had planned to drag my heels for a couple of days and run up the old expense account, like always, but I couldn't waste no time after hearin' that, so I slipped the kid a fin to let me deliver the stuff myself then called my client to meet me there. Piece a cake. When the old broad opened the door to get her prescription, zap!

Jack: *(tightly controlled)* You didn't hurt her none, did you?

Roscoe: Well, she started kickin' up a ruckus, so her son gave her some kinda calm-down shot while the wife and I held her. *(dramatically lecherous)* Ver-ron-ic-ah! That babe had a set you wouldn't believe! *(gestures)* Then, it was sleepy bye for the old gal. I love them old broads. Easy to handle.

Jack: *(barely manages to conceal his fury)* So . . . where did they take her?

Roscoe: *(lighting a cigarette)* Who knows; who cares? Some funny farm, I guess. They said she was crazy. What's another old broad, more or less, anyway? Who needs 'em? Boy did she holler at first! *(laughs)* Kept yellin' for someone named . . . Anna. Say, where's that beer?

Jack: Did ya catch the name of the place they took her to?

Roscoe: *(slightly annoyed, but trying to hold onto his jubilent mood)* Hey, I told you. I don't know and I don't care. You said you didn't know that old broad. What's it to you?

Jack: Maybe I know her, and maybe I don't. Maybe I just don't like folks bein' mean to old ladies. My ma's an old lady.

Roscoe: So's mine, so what? *(getting mad)* Say, I didn't need to tell you my business. I thought we was on the same wave length, you know, *(hitches at his pants)* both of us men of the world, and all . . .

Jack: *(snorts)* Think again, creep.

Roscoe: *(offended)* All right. Have it your way, Mac. *(his feelings are hurt)* I don't wanna talk no more. Gimme my friggin' beer.

Jack: *(furious)* I just remembered, we ain't got no more beer!

Roscoe: *(puzzled)* What the hell's goin' on? Ain't you in business here?

Jack: Can't you hear good, "Mac"? I said we ain't got no beer.

Roscoe: *(points)* Hell, I can see it from here.

Jack: Well, your eyes ain't working so good, "Mac". I think you're seeing things, "Mac". As a matter of fact, I don't like your looks!

Roscoe: *(shocked)* What the hell are you talking about?

Jack: You been hanging around here all day, ain't ya? Just waiting for me to close up. I know your kind. You better get your ass out of here right now, "Mac".

Roscoe: Goddamn! What's goin' on! You're off your rocker. All's I wanted was a beer. I dunno what you're so damn hot about. We was just talkin' . . .

Jack: Get the hell outta my place, mister. *(comes around the counter, pulling off his apron as he comes, ready to fight)* I don't want your business *(starts pushing Roscoe toward the door)*

Roscoe: What the friggin' hell is goin' on around here? Get your hands offa me, you creep!

Jack spins Roscoe around and gives him the bum's rush out the door. They ad lib. Jack locks the door. Through the window, we see a bewildered Roscoe get up and brush himself off. Inside, Jack reaches under the counter and locates a sawed-off baseball bat. He shows it to Roscoe through the window. Jack is almost crying. Roscoe makes a few threatening gestures, then gives Jack the finger and leaves.

Jack: *(against the window)* Get the hell outta here, you worthless bum. *(wipes his eyes, really crying)* Goddamned. Look at me. What the hell am I doing? That poor old dame! What's gonna become of her now?

The lights dim as the **Scene Ends.**

Act Two, Scene Three

It is now Thanksgiving time at the diner. There are typical Thanksgiving decorations around the place, cardboard pilgrims, etc. The bushes outside the window are topped with snow. The glass looks frosted. The light outside is grey and cold. The wall clock says 2:57. There are no other customers. Jack is seated at the booth beside Anna. She is still wearing her coat and scarf. She looks devastated. A battered cardboard shoe-box is on the table in front of her. Jack is trying to comfort Anna, but she is in a state of semi-shock and doesn't respond. She has been weeping and cluches a soggy tissue in one hand. Jack pats her awkwardly.

Jack: Gosh, I wish I could do something to help. Would you like some tea? It would warm you up.

Anna shakes her head "no". The door opens and Virginia hurries in, shivering from the cold.

Virginia: Oh, Anna, dear, I'm so sorry.

Jack hops up, glad to have help with the unhappy woman and Virginia slides onto the bench beside Anna. Anna leans her head against Virginia's shoulder.

Anna: I didn't even get to see her.

Virginia: When did it happen?

Anna: Five days ago. And I didn't even know.

Jack: *(to Virginia)* I'm sure glad you got here. Miz Brodzienski. I couldn't get her to go back home or nothin'. She didn't want to go by herself and I couldn't leave the place. I hope you don't mind that I called you.

Virginia: Of course not, you did the right thing, Mr. Moore.

Anna: I just keep thinking that she'll come walking right through that door again, just like she did before . . .

Virginia: No, dear. She won't do that. Not this time.

Anna: I just can't believe it.

Virginia: I can't either. It's just awful.

Jack: I'm gonna fix you both some nice tea. *(Jack heads behind the counter and begins to work.)*

Anna: If only she'd been able to write to me sooner.

Virginia: She did the best she could . . .

Anna: They kept her sedated most of the time, so she couldn't do anything.

Jack: Those jerks oughta be shot. What kinda people are they?

Anna: The minute I got the letter . . . note, really, all it said was; "I'm at Upton General, come get me if you can. Love Bea." . . . I went right over there.

Virginia: But Upton's a hospital. I thought they put her in a mental ward?

Anna: shakes her head, crying more) I don't know. I don't know. All I know is she's gone.

Virginia: Did she leave you a letter . . . or anything?

Anna: *(shakes her head)* Nothing. This is all she left me.

Anna opens the shoebox the reveals Bea's old red house slippers.

Anna: *(continues)* Just these old shoes. They were holding for me at the desk, with my name on the box. Her old slippers.
Anna puts the shoes back in the box and closes the lid. Jack brings the cups of tea to the table and puts one in front of each lady.

Jack: I made you one, too, Miz Brodzienski.

Virginia: Thank you, Mr. Moore.

Anna: We had such grand times. *(remembering fondly)* She always tried to make me laugh. Gosh, how we laughed! *(dabs her eyes)* Bea always said she'd get the last laugh on Sonny. But I guess she isn't going to. Not this time.

Jack: She was some nice lady. Always so jolly. Always leaving me them tips.

Virginia: How old was she, anyway? I never was sure.

Anna: She was a lot older than she looked. Almost 80, I think. She had a face lift about ten years ago because her husband wanted her to. *(sobs)* She had such clever ways of doing things. Like poking the orange peelings down the disposal, so the house would smell nice when we ran it, and putting a clothes pin on the potato chip bag after we opened it so they would stay fresh.

Jack: She was full of good ideas. Remember the carrot cake? I still make it that way.

Virginia: I remember how she stole her get-away money out of her daughter-in-law's purse.

Jack: And stuffed it in the toe of her slippers so she wouldn't find it, and came in here with only one slipper on . . .

The three suddenly have the same thought and fix their attention on the shoe box. They realize the thought is shared and look at each other, wondering.

Jack: Say, you don't suppose . . .?

Virginia: Do you think . . .?

They all grab for the shoe box. Anna tears the top off and snatches up one shoe. She sticks her hand inside and after a beat, wilts visible as she withdraws it, empty. She starts to reach for the other shoe but just can't bring herself to pick it up.

Jack: If she left a note, that's where it's gonna be. Go on, Miz Kranze. See if it's in there.

Virginia: Go on, Anna.

Anna reaches into the other slipper and finds something. Her face breaks into a smile and then she crumbles and begins to cry again.

Virginia: I hear paper. There's something in there. Pull it out!

Anna: Oh, I can't stand it! I'm afraid to look! What if it's just a bill from the dry cleaners or a shopping list? I can't bear it. I never even got to tell her good-bye!

Virginia takes the slipper from Anna's limp hand.

Virginia: Here, give it to me. We've got to know. *(She pulls out a small envelope.)* Look!

Jack: I'll be damned. A letter.

Virginia: It's addressed to you, Anna. Here.

Anna: *(wiping her eyes)* A letter? It's really a letter?

Jack: *(admiringly)* That Bea. What a foxy dame. She knew we'd find it.

Anna takes the envelope, looks at it lovingly then carefully opens it with a table knife. She withdraws a sheet of paper and opens it on the smoothing out the wrinkles tenderly.

Anna: *(reads)* "Dear Anna, *(her voice breaks and she dabs at her eyes before continuing)* If you are reading this, I must be dead. *(sobs)* I knew it was coming for a long time. There never was any hope. I just didn't want to end up all full to tubes and wires so I ran away. *(struggles to continue)*
"I wanted to have one last bit of fun and you sure helped me do it. I had the best time I had in years after I found you.
The day you asked me to come home with you was the best day of my life. You sure took a chance on a stranger, but I'm so glad you did.
"I'd like to leave you with some big important "last words", but I can't think of any. My friend, Raoul, the male night nurse is waiting to take this note and hide it in my slippers to give to you later. I want to finish it now because I'm not all fuzzed up tonight. They call it a remission, but they don't say how long it will last.
"Anyway, there is one thing I want to say. Remember the Brooklyn Promise you made me . . . that you would get out and have fun? I expect you to keep that promise, Anna. *(sobs)* Have all the fun you can, every minute of every day. This is the only life you've got, so enjoy it while you can. And laugh a lot, you've got such a lovely laugh. *(sobs)* And every now and then, think of me, your loving friend, Bea."

Anna breaks down completely and covers her face with her hands, sobbing. Virginia picks up the letter and scans it.

Virginia: Wait, there's more. You didn't read the P.S. *(reading)* "P.S. Write to Herr Gottsmidth, International Bank of Switzerland, Geneva and give him this number." There's a big long number here. "He will tell you much interest you've earned on the joint bank account I opened for us there last month. It has an automatic survivorship clause, and Sonny can't touch it. It should be enough to pay off your apartment. Use the rest any way you want to . . . as long as you have fun with it. Love, Bea." – My God, Anna! She opened you a Swiss bank account! You're rich!

Anna: *(dazed)* What?

Virginia: Bea. She left you her money . . . in a way her son-in-law can't get at it . . . a secret Swiss bank account! What a fox!

Jack: I heard about them Swiss accounts. All the big time crooks and politicians have em.

Virginia: You're rich!

Anna: *(dazed)* Why did she so that?

Virginia: She loved you, Anna.

Jack: You took a chance on her when she really needed it. It's her way of paying you back.

Anna: But I didn't expect anything . . .

Virginia: Of course not, that's what makes it so perfect.

Jack: And Bea had her last laugh, after all.

Virginia: She didn't want Sonny to get his hands on her money.

Anna: *(still dazed)* It must be thousands . . .

Virginia: *(laughs)* At least, if a month's interest will pay off your apartment!

Anna: It's in my name?

Virginia: That's what this letter says. You were her best friend. She wanted you to have it.

Anna: I just can't believe it.

Virginia: Now you've got no excuse at all. You've got to turn over a new leaf. Go places. Do things. You'll have plenty of money to do whatever you want.

Jack: Hawaii here you come!

Anna: *(sobs)* Oh, it wouldn't be the same without Bea.

Virginia: *(pats her hand)* No. Not the same. But you go ahead and do it anyway.

Jack: You bet, Miz Kranze. It's what Bea wanted.

Anna: *(warming to the idea)* Hawaii. Do you really think I could? I was really dreading another holiday season here, by myself. I hate the cold so much.

Virginia: Well, what are you waiting for? Thanks to Bea, you can just grab a suitcase, or better yet, buy a new one . . . jump on a plane and GO!

Jack: You'll make lots of new friends. Those places are full of nice retired folks. You'll have a great time.

Anna: Well . . .

Virginia: Don't fret about it, just do it.

Anna: Well . . .

Jack: Go for it, Miz Kranze. This is your chance. Live your life, like Bea said.

Jack: Go for it, Miz Kranze. This is your chance. Live your life, like Bea said.

Anna: All right! I will. *(smiles bravely)* It's what Bea would want me to do, and after all, I can't break a Brooklyn Promise!

CURTAIN

The Challenge of Bureaucracy

by Carole Glickfield

The Challenge of Bureaucracy

by Carole Glickfield

Cast List
Finney   Telephone voices #1 – 4

The Challenge of Bureaucracy

by Carole Glickfield

A Telephone Sketch

Finney: *(mumbles to herself as she dials phone, phone rings and a spot lights worker at desk)*

Worker #1: Hellooooo.

Finney: Hello . . . is this the government?

Worker #1: You have reached Department 3A-dash-nine. This is the rehabilitative relocations unit for block grant recipients within Region nine.

Finney: That's the government alright. Listen, I'm an old lady and I have a problem. My landlord is going to evict me because I'm behind in my rent, because my Social Security check is late, and I don't have any food in the house.

Worker #1: I'm sorry. Financial and dietary evaluations are not within the purview of my sectional expertise.

Finney: *(long pause)* I'd ask you to repeat that, but I don't think it would get any better the second time around.

Worker #1: Your problem is outside my jurisdiction. Let me refer you to another number. Call 355-4356. That's a multi-purpose senior center which receives funding under the Older Americans Act for access and gap-filling services.

Finney: Gap-filling?

Worker #1: Yes, gap-filling.

Finney: Well, I suppose you could say there's a gap in my income. And I sure need someone to fill it. Thank you. *(hangs up and dials new number)*

As Finney dials, spot light on Worker #1 blacks out, phone rings and another spot lights the second worker at her desk.

Worker #2: *(picks up phone)* Silver Retirees and Golden Pensioners Leisure Activities Center . . . good morning!

Finney: Good morning. I need help.

Worker #2: That's why we're here. Do you need a ride to your Silver Retirees and Golden Pensioners Leisure Activity Center?

Finney: No. I need my Social Security check which has been lost . . . my landlord is going to evict me . . . and I don't have any food in the house.

Worker #2: Oh, my! You mean you're not going to be joining us for leisure crafts this afternoon?

Finney: I very much doubt it.

Worker #2: You should have a hobby, you know. Something to occupy your time.

Finney: I do have a hobby. It's trying to locate Social Security checks, avoiding being evicted, and trying not to starve to death.

Worker #2: Well, as long as you're happy. That's what counts. Happiness is the natural margarine of the universe, and we're here to spread it.

Finney: Who do I call for help?

Worker #2: Oh. Yes. Well, let's see. *(flips through pad)* Golden Roamers Senior Center . . . White Panthers . . . Pepper Nutrition Program . . . Free Temperature taking . . . Toe-nail clipping . . . Ah! Here it is . . . Call 945-3301. That's Problem Senior Citizens.

Finney: I'm not a problem senior citizen. I'm a senior citizen with a problem. Goodbye. *(hangs up and dials number)*

As Finney dials, spot on Worker #2 blacks out. Phone rings, another spot lights Worker #3 at her desk.

Worker #3: Hello. This is Problem Senior Citizens. May we help you?

Finney: We? Is somebody else listening in on this conversation?

Worker #3: No, no. Just an expression.

Finney: Look, lady, my Social Security check is late . . . my landlord is going to evict me . . . I'm starving to death . . .

Worker #3: I see. Alright, when was your last Social Security check?

Finney: Three months ago.

Worker #3: When was your last meal?

Finney: Yesterday noon.

Worker #3: When was your last birthday?

Finney: Seventy-three

Worker #3: And sex?

Finney: March 10th, 1957

Worker #3: What?

Finney: About 11:30 in the evening.

Worker #3: I mean, are you male or female?

Finney: Female.

Worker #3: Are you Caucasian, Hispanic, Black, Asian or other?

Finney: What's other?

Worker #3: Not Caucasian. Not Hispanic. Not Black. Not Asian. What are you?

Finney: Hungry.

Worker #3: Ah yes, Hungarian. That would be white, wouldn't it?

Finney: Can you help me or can't you?

Worker #3: Do you qualify for food stamps? Is your income below $316 per month?

Finney: It's zero right now. If my check comes, it'll be $295, that's all I have.

Worker #3: What are your assets?

Finney: Perserverence . . . my looks . . .

Worker #3: Money in the bank? Other income?

Finney: Look, if I were a rich lady, would I be talking to you?

Worker #3: Yes. Well, why don't you let me process your claim for food stamps. You could get them in a matter of weeks.

Finney: You want me to be hungry for a matter of weeks? I need my Social Security check now! I don't want to be evicted . . . I don't want to starve to death!

Worker #3: Hmm . . . You do have a multiplicity of problems. Let me just punch this all into the computer and see what we get. Age 73, female, white, food stamps, eviction . . .

Finney: What does the damn thing say?

Worker #3: Ah . . . here we go. For information about late Social Security checks, call you Social Security ombudsman. For food stamps call the U.S. Department of Agriculture. For all landlord-tenant problems call the Tenants Protective Association . . . for sex counselling, call Planned Parenthood . . .

Finney: What? Where should I call?

Worker #3: Well, it's 5 o'clock. Why don't you call me back Monday morning and I'll give you the telephone numbers. (*hangs up*)

Spotlight on worker blacks out. Finney stares at the phone in her hand and then puts it down with a vast sigh. A moment of silence goes by.

Finney: (*looking up prayerfully*) Lord . . . Oh Lord Almighty . . . are you up there? Can you hear me, Lord? I'll never get into any kind of trouble again! I'll reform, Lord. Can you hear me, Lord? This is Mabel Finney . . .

Lord: *(voice from offstage)* This is the Lord . . . *(thunder off)* I am sorry that I couldn't be here to take your call. At the sound of the tone, please leave your name, number, and religious persuasion, and I'll get back to you first thing Monday morning. This is a recording . . . this is a recording . . . this is a recording . . .

As Finney stares at phone in horror. . .

BLACKOUT

The Day
They Kidnapped Blanche
by Ann Pugh and Katy Dacus

The Day They Kidnapped Blanche

by Ann Pugh and Katy Dacus

Cast List

Blanche	Ruby	Mrs. Sloane
Brent	Billy	Sol
Devon		

The Day They Kidnapped Blanche

by Ann Pugh and Katy Dacus

SCENE ONE

A sign hanging over the entrance to the Mid-Cities Senior Community Center reads, "USED CAR FOR SALE / Presented by Mid-Cities / Senior Citizens Drama Club / Matinee completely sold out. / Evening tickets at box office." A bike rack with a tandem bike is to the right of the entrance. Left is Devon, a menacing-looking man seated on a park bench in an amber spotlight. He is dresses in a dark suit and dark hat that shadows his face. While pretending to be reading a newspaper with bold headlines, he is obviously casing the area – waiting and looking for someone. A slide of a newspaper headline reads, "Mid-Cities Chronicle / Nursing Home Residents Missing / Staff and Police Still Baffled." A second slide appears reading,
"NEIGHBORHOOD NOTES / This is the last day to catch the play "Used Car For Sale" presented by the Senior Citizens Drama Club at the Mid-Cities Senior Community Center on Park Ridge. The matinee is sold out, but evening performance tickets are still available. Curtain at 8:00 p.m.

Blanche enters briskly, followed by Brent. Devon, quite interested in their conversation, eavesdrops from behind the newspaper. Blanche is a handsome septuagenarian — agile, slender, obviously athletic. She wears well-tailored slacks, a turtle-neck pull-over, tennis shoes, and mannish oxford-cloth shirt tied casually about her waist. She slings a knapsack along as she laughingly approaches her bike. Brent, in his late 20's, is teasing her. They are great pals and enjoy their show-biz bantering despite their great age difference. They do not notice Devon.

Brent: *(Teasing, following Blanche)* What's your hurry, Blanche? I've got Hollywood on hold.

Blanche: Neil Simon again? What a pest he is!

Brent: Shall I tell him what I always do – David Merrick has first priority?

Blanche: *(laughing)* Don't forget ABC wants me to do the Farrah Fawcett role in the geriatric version of Charley's Angels.

Brent: You really should consider Neil Simon's offer. He is begging you to star in his latest zinger *(nudges Blanche meaningfully)* "Last of the Red Hot Grannies". *(makes clicking sound)*

Blanche: Hush your mouth! I'm far too young to play any grandmother role. *(imitating the age-sensitive star)* I'm not a day over 38. – – 48? *(Both laugh.)* I'll play any part so long as it doesn't promote porno or Polident. These are my own, *(indicating teeth)* and if you don't believe it. . .

51

Brent: I believe! *(changing mood to an almost scolding tone)* I saw on the call board that you're throwing the cast party.

Blanche: *(flippant)* You expected an engraved invitation?

Brent: You know what I mean. Let someone else do the party.

Blanche: Why?

Brent: You take on too much. Always do more than your share.

Blanche: I do exactly what I want to do. When did a little work ever hurt anyone?

Brent: But, Blanche. . .

Blanche: *(cutting him off gently)* Brent, dear, I've told you all along I intend to have the gang over tomorrow night. *(pats Brent on the cheek)* Not to worry. It's all taken care of. Lasagna's made and in the freezer. Sarah and Ruthie are doing salad. Cliff and Sam are bringing beer – which you, dear boy, will ice down in my bath tub. Simple.

Brent: You are something else!

Blanche: Yes, like what – a bossy old teacher?

Brent: You, Blanche, are one classy lady. I adore you, but we must stop meeting like this.

Blanche: I know. It's sheer madness. You know how gossipy show folks are. *(throws him a kiss)* Gotta run.

Brent: Why ride all that distance when I can have a sandwich sent in, and you can put your feet up and relax before tonight's show?

Blanche: Who's tired? I promised Ruthie I'd drop that stagecraft book by her place – and you know how Ruthie is! Who wants a soggy sandwich when you can have homemade soup at home. Besides, I need the exercise.

Brent: Just remember you do have a show tonight. Don't pick up a date on your way home, okay? *(looks at bike)* When are you gonna get rid of that big gas guzzler, anyhow? You need a new compact.

Blanche: When I'm too lazy to peddle about, I'll trade "Sadie" for a moped.

Brent: You're impossible! See you at the 'half hour'. *(exits)*

Blanche: *(kicks kick-stand up, and about to ride off when Devon moves over and blocks her exit)*

Devon: Blanche Sherwin? Are you Mrs. Sherwin? Can I talk to you a few minutes?

Blanche: *(politely correcting him)* May I. May I talk to you?

Devon: *(politely)* May I?

Blanche: You may. You may take one giant step.

Devon: What?

Blanche: The game, "May I" – Remember it? It helped kids remember proper grammar. Whatever happened to proper grammar? Was it thrown out with good manners, Mr. – ?

Devon: Oh, I'm sorry. Devon. Steve Devon.

Blanche: Half of your generation are.

Devon: Are what?

Blanche: Named Steve. The other half are Mikes. They were the most popular names of your generation. I have one of each. If you have a sister, she's Karen – or – Sharon.

Devon: (nods and agrees) Twins, Karen and Sharon. (Indicates bench) Can we sit here a minute?

Blanche: (always the teacher, politely nudging) May we sit. I was an English teacher.

Devon: Yes, I can believe that. A good one, too, I bet. You're one hell of an actress, Mrs. Sherwin. I saw your show three times.

Blanche: You did?

Devon: Yes. And I wanted to meet you. You were great in the part.

Blanche: Then it may interest you to know that role was written for a man. Brent, our director, felt it was so universal that it could just as easily be a woman. After all, loneliness is not sexually discriminating, is it? Nor racially, for that matter. Anyhow, thanks to Carlino, it works for an actress. He writes so beautifully. He has such sensitivity – such understanding of the elderly.

Devon: Who does?

Blanche: Carlino, the playwright. Lewis John Carlino. He wrote *Used Car for Sale*. He also wrote *The Great Santini*. Perhaps you saw the film? It won an Academy Award. (confused by Devon watching her and not replying) You did say you saw our play?

Devon: Three times.

Blanche: Yes, that's what I thought you said, but. . .

Devon: To tell you the truth, Mrs. Sherwin, I'm much more interested in you than in the play or the author.

Blanche: Oh, really? . . . I'm flattered, of course. But frankly I'm a bit confused. Are you for real? You're too mature for a stage-door-Johnny. – – You're not kinky are you? Never mind, at my age almost any approach is – interesting. Now if you'll excuse me, Mr. Devon, (making an effort to ride off) I must be going.

Devon: (blocking Blanche again) You bike here for every performance? You must be in good health.

Blanche: *(directly)* I'm blessed with good genes. *(She tries to dismiss Devon and ride off, but is stopped physically by his grabbing the handle bars. She is peeved.)* I beg your pardon!

Devon: I don't mean to alarm you. I have something important to discuss with you. Are you familiar with the nursing homes in this area?

Blanche: What are you doing? Drumming up new residents? I'm not ready for that. Deliver me from some pip squeak of a recreation director that thinks wearing silly hats and tooting kazoos is everybody's idea of a big time. Hell's bells, if he can't clear up his acne, he's not ready to handle the elderly.

Devon: I wish that were the biggest problem in caring for the elderly.

Blanche: Yes, you're quite right. I read about a place up state that can't even keep track of their residents. Two wandered away and have not been heard of yet. *(riding off)*

Devon: Maybe they didn't wander away. Maybe they were taken away. *(This stops Blanche. She turns back.)*

Who knows, they could be in another state. Perhaps dead.

Blanche: How horrible! Poor souls. It's so tragic for their families. Is one of them a relative?

Devon: No. There are no families. No close friends. Both were totally alone in the world. But somebody knew how to get their money.

Blanche: Goodness, how dreadful! I'm so sorry, Mr. Devon, but I really need to go. I've an errand to run, and I must eat supper before I return for tonight's performance. *(tries to leave)*

Devon: Are you physically strong, Mrs. Sherwin?

Blanche: *(a bit testy)* Yes, for my age! But why are you asking me all these questions? You sound like a detective in a TV series. You're too neat for Columbo. Are you with the government?

Devon: Exactly. FBI. *(shows identification badge)*

Blanche: *(almost haughty)* Are you investigating me? *(beat, then curiously)* What have I done?

Devon: For one thing, you turned back your Social Security.

Blanche: Well, it's my Social Security. I can turn it back if I want to. Besides, I don't need it. I'm not all that radical surely? Is it now a federal offense to turn it back?

Devon: No, but it is unique. It made quite an impression on our computer. The Bureau was curious. You've been under surveillance for over a week. The more we learned about you, the more convinced the Bureau was that you were right for an undercover assignment.

Blanche: You've got to be kidding!

54

Devon: How old are you?

Blanche: Shame on you! A gentleman never asks that question.

Devon: 68?

Blanche: *(flattered)* You're a doll! *(coyly)* Really 70 – that is – actually *(making a full confession)* 70 and a half.

Devon: *(Smiling)* 71 on December 19th at 4:23 p.m.

Blanche: My god, Big Brother knows everything!

Devon: Yep, we make it our business. Even your friend Brent doesn't know how many fillings you have. We do.

Blanche: Since you've been watching me so closely, does that mean you're tapping my phone?

Devon: Didn't need to. From day-one we knew you had all the right qualifications. You are exactly what we want – a lady who is – uh – *(hesitating)* well over 50 – that is a senior citizen – that is. . .

Blanche: *(enjoys watching him squirm)* Oh, go on, say it! I'm a septuagenarian. *(impressed)* My god, that's an immmpressive handle isn't it? Like sagitarian! Or valedictorian! Yes, there are decided advantages to growing older. Okay, so we've established the fact I've passed your minimum-age requirement. What else must I do to satisfy you and the "fellows at the Bureau"?

Devon: Be alert. Observant. Healthy. Able to work under pressure. Make quick decisions. And be a convincing actress – but not so well-known as to be easily recognizable.

Blanche: Yes. Well, you can safely say I'm one of the world's lesser known starlets. Now, my friend, just what is this gig? Is it dangerous? What is involved?

Devon: It can be extremely dangerous. I won't lie to you, but the degree of danger is lessened by your acting ability.

Blanche: Oh, keen! And suppose the Mata Hari of the Geritol set is not my role? *(thinking, then)* If I don't survive, promise me something. . .

Devon: Anything you say.

Blanche: When the Academy Awards nominate me for Best Supporting Actress *(pointedly)* posthumously, *(firmly)* don't let them put my middle name on the Oscar. I hate it!

Devon: Does that mean you will accept the assignment?

Blanche: I'm hungry. I never make big decisions on an empty stomach. How does vegetable soup, hot bread, and Chablis sound?

Devon: Great.

Blanche: *(indicating back seat of her bike)* Hop on. Let's go!

   They ride off stage. **BLACKOUT.**

SCENE TWO

In a corridor of a Nursing Home one week later. An early afternoon. Set piece with bulletin board. Logo reads "Activities"

Ruby, a big hulk of a nurse, enters with a tray of medication. Looking about furtively and spotting no one in sight, she plops her big buttocks atop a desk, picks up the phone and dials.

Ruby: That you, Charlene? How's tricks? *(laughs coarsly)* . . . What with the convention an' all, I expect y'all had a little action over there . . . No kiddin'? Broken glass and the whole bit, huh? Is Duke around, or is he next door pumpin' iron? . . . Well, tell him Big Mamma's on the phone . . . *(scratches)* Hello, Duke darlin'. Sure been missin. you. Did you win at poker last night? . . . Whatta shame. If Big Mamma'd have been there you'd of had one long winnin' streak, but never mind, Lover, our luck's about to change. I gotta surprise for you. Remember that big, lavendar Caddylac we saw last week? *(enticingly)* If you're sweet to Ruby, mebbe she's got a way of gettin' it for you . . . *(testy)* Like hell, I'm kiddin'! I'm comin' into some big bucks! . . . From an ol' uncle back in Kansas, that's who . . . Yeah! He jest kicked off. An' guess who's his only livin' relative? . . . You got it, Ace, Your Big Mamma. Gotta go on ut to Kansas for a few days to settle the stuff an' get my money. I been thinkin' wouldn't it be a good time for a honeymoon? I still got them travel folders on *(mispronouncing)* Hawaya. *(not noticing entrance of Billy and Blanche, she continues conversation)*

Billy, an ignorant and cocky male attendant, brings on Blanche in a wheel chair. She is a changed person, helpless and senile in a droopy bathrobe, pajamas, and house slippers. Her hair is dis-sheveled. She wears a hearing aid. She nervously twists and fools with it constantly.

Ruby: *(into phone in a seductive come-hither tone)* I could send you a plane ticket so's we could get together in L.A. . . . Well, don't think about it too long, Lover, 'cause I might jest make some other plans! *(slams down phone)*

Billy: *(scolding in an immature way)* No, No, No! Not supposed to use the phone for personal calls.

Ruby: *(whirls around and snaps)* Shut up! *(crossing to Blanche, turns on the sugar)* Well, how are we doin' today, Blanche, honey? Did we have our therapy? *(no reaction from Blanche, who is in her own world)* Well, never mind, honey, we'll feel better after we take our little ride. *(wheels Blanche out of the way and out of ear shot. Blanche plays with her hearing aid absently, out of habit.)*

Blanche: *(singing in a child-like senile manner to tune of "Mulberry Bush")* "This is the way we take our ride, take our ride, take our ride" *(voice trails off incoherently)*

Ruby: *(impatiently)* There she goes again! Ever now an' then the old girl gets that hearin' aid workin' an' catches jest enough to start her off on that sing-song crap.

Blanche: *(continuing incoherently for the most part)* "This is the day we take our ride, take our ride, take our ride".

Billy: She sure don't hear much tho', does she?

Ruby: Naw. The doctor he said she keeps her hearin' aid broke most of the time. She was a music teacher, an' half the time she thinks she's back in the second grade. He said not to worry about tryin' to keep it fixed, 'cause she don't know what's goin' on anyhow.

Billy: Yeah, a real loonie, that one! Why do you wanna bother to take her, anyhow? Seems like she's a lot of trouble.

Ruby: For her kind of money I can put up with plenty of trouble. That old dame's loaded. I mean really loaded!

Billy: Yeah?

Ruby: I sure got lucky on that one.

Billy: How come?

Ruby: A neighbor found her after a stroke an' brought her here 'cause she don't have no family or nothin'. She's putty in my hands. I can handle her kind real good. *(to Blanche in a little girl voice)* Mrs. Sherwin, this is report card day. Mrs. Sherwin, you gonna sign little Ruby's report card so we can go on the nice trip?

Billy: What's this report card thing? Why she's gonna sign a report card?

Ruby: *(impatiently)* A check, you dolt! She's gonna sign her name on a check – a nice fat check – which I'm gonna cash on the way out of town.

Billy: Oh, yeah! I see! She thinks – Gee, I never would 'uv though of that.

Ruby: Or anything else, dummie. You jest leave the thinkin' to Ruby.

Billy: When do I get my money? You promised you'd pay me today.

Ruby: Soon as we go by the bank on our way to – never mind where. Soon as I go by the bank and cash their checks.

Blanche: *(Singing)* "The king was in his counting house counting out his money. The queen was in her parlor eating bread and honey."

Ruby: You did get the van like I told you, didn't you?

Billy: *(cocky)* No.

Ruby: *(angrily)* I knew it! You stupid son of a – . You never get anythin' right. I should 'uv taken care of that myself.

Billy: Now, hold on to your horses, Ruby! Jest who do you think yer callin' stupid? I'll have you know I got us a van. It's a beaut! With a cab separate from the back. A CB an' everything. . .

Ruby: That's more like it. Where'd you get it?

Billy: From a buddy – belongs to his old man, who don't need it for a couple of days cause he's shut down his bakery shop for repairs. It's brand new – only used it for deliveries a couple of weeks.

Ruby: *(raising voice)* A baker's van? Not a baker's van!

Blanche: *(singing)* "Pat-a-cake, pat-a-cake, baker's van. Bake me a cake as fast as you can". *(They ignore Blanche, she repeats, trailing off)*

Ruby: *(signs disgusted)* Well, it sure better be right.

Billy: It is! It's got a tape deck an' them fancy sun screens on the windows so's nobody kin see in. Nobody'll know the old crazies are back there, an' we won't have to listen to 'em up in the cab. It's spiffy as hell.

Ruby: You better 'uv worked it right. I don't want to have to make up no stories to alibi for stolen stuff. Too much at stake to fool with a hot car.

Billy: It ain't hot! I told you I had connections. This guy – my buddy – owes me a favor. I help him unload Mexican grass. I borrowed his van all legal with papers. He thinks I'm movin' some furniture for my step mother.

Ruby: *(sighing impatiently)* Okay. Mebbe you did it right.

Billy: What I done was a lot more legal than what you done to get me hired on here. Sure hope nobody finds out about them job placement forms you faked.

Ruby: *(threateningly)* They better not find out! Cause if they do, I'll know who blabbed!

Billy: Now, Ruby, you know I wouldn't do nothin' to mess up this sweet deal. Ruby, sugar, you know me.

Blanche: *(singing absently)* "Violets are blue. Ruby is sweet and so are you." *(They ignore her.)*

Ruby: Yeah! I sure do. You'd sell your own mother fer a buck, but it is a sweet deal. And doncha forget it!

Billy: I ain't about to. Hey, we gotta decide what time we're shovin' off, and how many's goin'. Is it two or three?

Ruby: I'll decide how many. I make the decisions. You jest have the van where it's supposed to be. I'll handle the rest. I'll have the three of them ready to –

Billy: Three? All three, huh?

Blanche: *(singing unnoticed)* "Three blind mice, three blind mice. See how – "

Ruby: *(to Billy)* That's what I said. I'll have them ready to roll at one o'clock. Get that? One o'clock on the dot! Don't be late.

Blanche: *(singing)* "Hickory Dickory Dock. The mouse ran up the clock – The clock struck *one*, and down they run –

Billy: So you talked the old salesman into buyin' in? How about that!

Ruby: Finally! What a fight that was! Wanted to know every little thing about them condos. When he found out Mrs. Sloan was buyin' he was afraid he was gonna miss out on somethin'. Mainly I hooked him when I told him there was a kosher kitchen.

Billy: Old lady Sloane didn't put up a ruckus? I figured her to sniff around like a bird dog.

Ruby: Jest you leave everthing to me. I know what I'm doin' – I know jest what to promise these old codgers. Mrs. Sloane wants a pretty place with a patio like she had back in San Diego, so she gets it – complete with pots of geraniums.

Billy: You don't think she's on to us, do you?

Ruby: Naw! She's so busy playing Florence Nightingale to Blanche and Mother Superior to Sol that she can't think of nothin' else. She bought the whole thing – hook, line, and sinker. Thinks she's movin' into a new home in Utopia.

Billy: U-whatsia? *(voice raised)* I thought we was goin' to that cabin you told me about up in Mac Donald County.

Ruby: Shut up, you fool!

Blanche: *(singing)* "Old Mac Donald had a farm ee-ii-ee-ii-o. Old Mac Donald had a farm, and on that farm – *(voice trails on)*

Ruby: *(to Billy)* You dolt! Keep your voice down! I'll tell you what you need to know when you need to know it, an' not before. *(looks at watch)* Okay, now's the time to make our move. By the time the head nurse finds them gone an' notifies the supervisor, our shift will be over. An' nobody'll be the wiser until we put distance betwen us the this place. You got the van gassed up an' ready to travel?

Billy: Yeah, did everthing jest like you told me.

Ruby: Now remember, don't act scared, no matter what. If Sol starts talkin', no matter what he says, you jest smile an' keep your trap shut, 'cause nobody believes that old geezer anyhow.

Billy: First we get our money? We go by the bank an' get our money?

Ruby: A condo owner in a baker's van? Stupid! Of course not. You go on out highway 30 – Interstate 30.

Blanche: *(singing, unnoticed)* "Thirty days has September – *(confused)* April – *(starts again)* Thirty days has November – *(gives up)*

Ruby: That's east of town. Park at the flea market, an' wait for me. There's so many vans at the flea market nobody will

Blanche: *(singing)* "To market, to market, to buy a fine pig – "

Ruby: *(continues)* notice one more. It's east of here, you know, east of town. *(pointing)* That way is east.

Billy: *(snapping)* I know which way is east!

Blanche: *(confused, reacts to his loud tone)* Easter? *(sings)* "Here comes Peter Cotton Tail hopping down the Easter bunny trail."

Ruby: I'll circle by the bank in my car. Got it all planned to be there right at the rush hour.

Billy: What if they won't cash them checks?

Ruby: Don't worry, I been butterin' up a little teller who's jest fresh out of high school. Took her to lunch one day an' showed her pictures of my classy new condo nursin' home – confided in her that some patients from here would be buyin' their own places soon. That kid ain't dry behind the ears yet, so when I go to her window with the checks, it'll be a piece of cake!

Lights squeeze out, lingering a few seconds on Blanche as a pin spot picks up Devon speaking over a walkie-talkie.

Devon: *(into walkie-talkie)* Okay, men, we got it all! Turner, your hearing aid idea worked fine. Three hostages. Travelling in a bakery van. Moving out at one o'clock. Travelling east on Interstate 30 toward Mac Donald County. Two stops, apparently – the bank and a market – probably the flea market is the rendezvous spot. Ruby is a tough cookie – capable of murder. Repeat: Don't lose them! You're tailing in three vehicles and a motor cycle? . . . Good! I don't want anything to happen to Mrs. Sherwin, she's no kid and she's risking her neck for us. She's real gutsy, that lady. One of a kind! All the king's horses and all the king's men couldn't put that Blanche together again.

BLACKOUT

SCENE THREE

Blue lights on center stage. Two grimy set pieces with one practical door each in need of repair and paint, a battered old kitchen table, and two broken-down chairs suggest a dirty old abandoned cabin. Entrance is closed. A narrow door leads to a bathroom. It is late afternoon the same day.

The pitiful and senile Blanche, as seen in the nursing home, sits languishing in a wheelchair. Sol, a neat but sullen old man wears trousers, shirt, dark cardigan sweater, white socks, house shoes, and wire-frame glasses, also in a wheel chair. He has a cane. Mrs. Sloane, a well-groomed elderly lady in an expensive blouse, skirt, jacket, British walking shoes, pearl jewelry, and up-to-date reading glasses, enters from the bathroom. She is trying to manage her aluminum walker while shaking her dripping hands in disgust.

Mrs. Sloane: *(exasperated)* What a filthy bathroom! Not only is there no soap, there are no clean towels! Only a "primitive thing" that I simply could not bring myself to touch. Why would we ever stop here, Mr. Finkelstein? Any service station would have been cleaner. Didn't you hear me ask them to stop an hour ago?

Sol: *(Yiddish dialect, long-suffering tone)* I heard you, Mrs. Sloane. Always I'm hearing you. Sol Finkelstein doesn't have a hearing problem. *(suddenly, addressing god)* Don't be getting any ideas. Arthritis in the knees is enough already.

Mrs. Sloane: What on earth can be taking so long?

Sol: *(shrugs)* Something about the van. The transmission-carburator. A mechanic, I'm not.

Mrs. Sloane: But why are we waiting here?

Sol: Better to be waiting in this place than riding in the back end of that fugitive from a schlock yard! What a ride, already! Oy, mine stomach is completely twisted! We should only trade cars altogether. Some crummy van! Some crummy driver! Lately my heartburn has arthritis!

Mrs. Sloane: Mr. Finkelstein, allow me to give you a mint to settle your *(ladylike)* uh – problem. *(tries to find something in her handbag)*

Sol: *(dismissing her idea)* Mrs. Sloane, I don't need your lady-like mints. Call *(indicating the entrance door)* Mrs. Ruby Burns to bring you a towel. And she could also give me some relief.

Mrs. Sloane: *(tries the door which won't open)* It's stuck.

Sol: *(disbelieving and argumentative)* Why should it be stuck?

Mrs. Sloane: I'm sure I don't know that, Mr. Finkelstein, but it is stuck.

Sol: *(disgusted, wheeling his chair to the door)* Here, let me see. You probably turned the wrong way. Let me turn the knob. I'll get it open. *(fumbles with knob, but it won't budge)*

Blanche: in the normal voice of scene 1 with a quiet, sensible tone) The door is locked.

Sol: *(dismissing Blanche's contribution)* Another news bulletin from "the Babbler."

Mrs. Sloane: *(to Blanche, soothingly)* It's alright, Blanche. The door is only stuck – probably needs oil.

Blanche: *(whipping out a walkie-talkie from under her robe. Firmly but quietly)* No, the door is locked. *(Blanche jerks out the antenna as Mrs. Sloane and Sol watch in confused panic, then speaks into the mouthpiece.)* Devon, Humpty Dumpty here! We seem to have arrived at our destination – a deserted cabin. Two miles after a school playground, there is fresh gravel on the highway, then a turn left onto a paved road. After a rickety bridge take an easy turn right. Continue about a mile. Cross over a cattle-guard and make a sharp turn right. Cabin is down a little ravine in wooded area. Only two rooms, but possibly some out-buildings back in the trees. I thought I saw a roof. No dogs, and no signs of other hostages. *(Sol and Mrs. Sloane are terrified – especially at the word "hostages".)* Any instructions? . . . *(nods)* Roger. Over and out. *(quickly closes down the walkie-talkie and hides it under robe.)*

Sol: We're hostages? Why?

Mrs. Sloane: *(terrified)* How dreadful of you! I can't believe it! I just can't believe such a thing can –

Sol: *(impatiently)* What's not to believe? We're here. That door is locked. You saw her talk over that "talkie-walkie" machine. *(to Blanche)* Such a trick you played with your funny songs and no hearing. What are you? The head godmother of some racket? What kind of an outfit is this that would take us hostage? Oy, mine stomach!

Mrs. Sloane: *(tearfully to Blanche)* How could you be involved in such a terrible thing? What made you do it? How I misjudged you. I thought were a woman of breeding.

Blanche: I don't want to alarm you, my dears, but I must tell you we have been kidnapped. You, me, all of us. *(getting out of wheelchair gingerly)* I'll explain everything, but first let me get some circulation in my backside. *(Sol and Mrs. Sloane are shocked to see Blanche stand and stretch.)* What a relief to get out of that chair! *(moves over cautiously to listen for sounds behind the entry door)* They seem to be gone. Good, now I can loosen up. *(She whips off her bathrobe, revailing pajamas and does a brisk side-straddle-hop, followed by other exercises as Sol and Mrs. Sloane stare incredulously.)*

Sol: What are you? Some kind of a gym teather?

Blanche: *(exercising)* Actually, I am an English teacher. *(Mrs. Sloane is a bit less disturbed, and finds this acceptable)* . . . turned actress.

Mrs. Sloane: *(disapproving)* An actress. On the stage?

Sol: What's the matter? You couldn't get along with the school board? *(disdainfully)* Who makes a living acting?

Blanche: *(jogging)* I may not make any money, but my life is never dull. It beats sitting around counting my liver splotches. *(Mrs. Sloane self-consciously tries to conceal hers.)* My dears, whether you approve of life upon the wicked stage or not, my acting and yours may very well be the only way we can save our lives and possibly the lives of several others.

Sol: Who's this others? Ruby and Billy? Are they hostages?

Blanche: No, they are the kidnappers.

Mrs. Sloane: No, Blanche dear, you have things all mixed up. Ruby Burns supervises a lovely condo for senior citizens. She's taking us there.

Blanche: No, she isn't. There's no such place.

Mrs. Sloane: *(getting hand bag)* There most certainly is! See. . . *(gets out a brochure)* here it is. "The Golden Age Care Condos" It's a marvelous place with saunas, and a movie theatre, and classes in sculpture, and –

Sol: Even a kosher kitchen. See the little Star of David there?

Mrs. Sloane: It's a beautiful place on 30 acres with a battery-driven golf cart for each condo, and a staff that includes a full time doctor, nurses, a priest.

Sol: And a rabbi! Temple services every Friday night.

Blanche: My dears, forgive me for shattering your dreams, but there is no such place.

Sol: How can you say that? It's all there on that brochure. See? It says: "Ruby Burns, Supervisor, Golden Age Care Condos."

Mrs. Sloane: *(nodding agreement and reading brochure)* "The newest concept in apartment living for senior citizens."

Blanche: It's a fake.

Sol: *(indignant)* How can it be a fake? It's all there! See the photographs of the buildings? And there – there's a golf cart with people in it. That's no artist drawing; that's a genuine photograph!

Blanche: Yes, of a condo over in Sarasota, Florida. Out on the Armand's Key. *(digs a brochure from robe pocket)* Here is the very same brochure before Ruby's doctoring.

Sol: Doctoring? What's this doctoring?

Blanche: It's easy to do. It's called an overprint. A printer just added a few lies, like Ruby's name and a fictitious address. See, the color of the ink is different. This blue ink is just a tad lighter than the blue throughout.

Sol: *(examining brochure carefully)*Oy, she's right. It is!

Mrs. Sloane: But we paid for condos there. I bought one. Sol bought one. I thought you bought one.

Blanche: Yes, I hoped everyone would think so. You gave Ruby a lot of money for something that does not exist. So did patients from another retirement home over in Hillsdale. That's why I'm here. I'm a plant.

Mrs. Sloane: *(confused)* A plant?

Blanche: I'm working with the FBI.

Sol: *(with disbelief)* So now she's a J. Edna Hoover! *(suspiciously)* What's the matter? You couldn't hold a steady job? *(Blanche smiles patiently.)*

Mrs. Sloane: How could a lady such as yourself become involved in such a sordid enterprise? Not to overlook the fact that you have placed Mr. Finkelstein and myself in a dangerous charade. I repeat, why would you do such a thing?

Blanche: I fully understand your fright and concern. There are risks, of course, but they can be lessened if we cooperate with each other.

Sol: *(exasperated)* So now she wants that I should be a James Bond! *(with a touch of nostalgic bravado)* You should have come to me thirty years ago. In that Essex I was a regular Humphrey Bogart . . . But I'm telling you, confidentially, *(taping wheel chair)* this slowed me down. A Jaguar XYZ, it ain't!

Mrs. Sloane: Surely, you're not expecting us to "play-act" when our lives are at stake. There's not enough ham in us for that, is there, Mr. Finkelstein?

Sol: *(with a gesture of protest)* No ham here! I'm one hundred percent kosher!

Mrs. Sloane: *(to Blanche)* I suppose creative people would stop at nothing to be in the spotlight, regardless of the consequences. Rather selfish motives, I should think.

Blanche: Oh, I guess there might be some ego involved. This role's a natural for me – perhaps one last chance to play the part of a lifetime and help my fellows at the same time.

Mrs. Sloane: I don't understand how playing a part could help your fellows.

Blanche: Do you realize why you are here? Out of all the people in the home, don't you find it strange that only you were selected to move to new quarters?

Sol: Money. It's always money. A fancy condo don't come cheap.

Blanche: Yes, money's important. You have the cash, and you're alone in the world. No one checks on your welfare or your finances. You receive no letters, no phone calls.

Mrs. Sloane: *(sadly)* That's true. I have only the one niece, who lives over in Saudi Arabia. She never bothers to send a postcard.

Blanche: And, Sol, I learned your only son is dead, isn't that so?

Sol: *(bitterly)* He's dead to me.

Mrs. Sloane: I don't understand. You had a son? You never told me.

Sol: What's to tell? He turned his back on his people. Married a gentile. They're both university professors. Intellectual big shots! My son, Norman, the professor! He's so smart he can't teach his son the Torah or give my grandson a decent Jewish name! What kind of a name is *(with disgust)* Shawn? *(the final hurt)* Thank g-d Esther didn't live to see our son forsake his people.

Blanche: I'm sorry, Sol. But you see that very thing – your estrangement from your son makes you an easy victim for criminals. All the more reason why those of us who can, must fight for ourselves, who will? Everyone has his own crusade and can't be bothered with ours. Our future is so short, we're hardly worth the trouble to some folks. That's the reason – *(interrupted)* Shh – listen. *(All three listen.)*

Ruby: *(offstage)* I told you to part the van out of sight. Instead, you park on a hill with the brake off, an' it rolls into a tree – Now, thanks to you, we really got car trouble!

Billy: Yeah? Well, mebbe this little delay's a good thing. We need to talk money again. I didn't know what we was into before we started. Now, I know it's worth more'n you're payin' me.

Ruby: You little slob! You wouldn't have this much if it wasn't fer me. No more talk! Or mebbe you'd like to walk on back to town?

Blanche: You hear that? Now there's no time for debate. You have a choice, be an actor – or a corpse! *(sound of door being unlocked. An unhappy Billy enters with stack of blankets.)*

Billy: *(muttering)* She's gonna cut me down once too often, an' I'm gonna let her *(with a threatening gesture)* have it! Who does she think she is, anyhow? I'd like to see her pull this off without me! Bossy old bitch! *(Sol and Mrs. Sloane react to rough language)*

Mrs. Sloane: *(dabbing at nose due to musty odor of blankets)* Mercy! What are you doing with those nasty ragged blankets? Surely, they're not intended for our use.

Billy: Hey, it's gonna be cold here tonight. You'll be glad you have 'em later.

Mrs. Sloane: Whatever do you mean "later"? Surely we aren't to be here much longer.

Billy: That depends . . .

Mrs. Sloane: Depends on what? I demand to be taken to a first class hotel if we aren't going directly to our condo.

Billy: Listen, your highness, you ain't callin' the shots here.

Mrs. Sloane: *(indignant)* Well, really, young man!

Sol: Billy, I think there's something you should know about Blanche. *(Blanche, unseen by Billy, reacts worriedly. Mrs. Sloane doesn't know what to think.)*

Billy: Yeah, what?

Sol: She's . . . *(hesitates, trying to make up his mind)* a rotten singer. *(Blanche is relieved; Mrs. Sloane is still confused)*

Billy: Yeah, I heard her singin'.

Sol: A day of her music is enough already! *(Sol and Mrs. Sloane exchange glances)* You think I'm going to listen to her all night? *(threatening)* Just wait till my son hears about this!

Billy: Aw, quit dreamin', old man. You ain't got no son!

Mrs. Sloane: *(eagerly)* Yes, he does! He lied about not having any relatives, because – *(interrupted)*

Sol: *(cutting her off)* So I lied! *(sadly)* Who could blame me? I was ashamed to tell about my son.

Billy: Yeah – why? Does he cheat on his income tax?

Sol: *(furtively)* Oy, worse than that. He's *(making a confession of the sordid truth)* with the Mafia.

Billy: He's what? *(laughing in ridicule)* What would an old geezer like you know about the Mafia?

Sol: You'd be surprised, – he's got a Newark connection. *(peering around himself)* Very close to a family – and I don't mean his relatives. He's a strike man! *(eye-balling Billy)* You know what that is, don't you?

Billy: *(getting concerned)* Ye – yeah, I think so. You mean your son's a hit man in the Mafia?

Sol: *(long suffering)* Such a disgrace! Even our rabbi won't speak to him. For years he's been doing it – scrubbing people out.

Billy: *(fearful)* You mean he really murders people?

Sol: *(nodding)* So often he bought stock in a cement factory.

Billy: *(with fast-talking cowardice)* Well, you know, I didn't have anything to do with this. It was all Ruby's idea.

Mrs. Sloane: Just exactly what is Ruby's idea? Are we to go to our condo this evening or not?

Billy: I don't know nothin' about her plan. I was jest hired to drive the van to your new place, an' that's all I know.

Blanche: *(firmly)* Well, if you don't want to spend the rest of your life in the penitentiary for kidnapping, you'd better cooperate with us.

Billy: *(shocked at this different and "in command" Blanche)* I thought you was – you mean you ain't – what kind of a game y'all playin'? Y'all tryin' to make trouble fer me?

Sol: You already got planty of trouble. Blanche is under the covers with the FBI. *(to Blanche)* Blanche, show him your talkie-walkie machine.

Blanche: *(whips out the walkie-talkie again, jerks up antenna, and speaks into it as Billy watches in fear and shock)* Right on target with Billy. He's reading us loud and clear. Over and out.

Billy: *(frightened)* Jeez – what is this?

Sol: We ain't finished with you yet. *(threatening)* Jest wait till J. Edgar Hoover and my son, "the strike man", close in! Then you'll see something! *(warning)* You'll be lucky you don't get caught in the "cross-wire".

Mrs. Sloan: *(not to be outdone)* And you pay attention. Furthermore, I come from a long like connected with – *(searching for something impressively awesome)* – jurisprudence! *(not having any idea what that is, Billy is very frightened)*

Blanche: If you want to save your hide, you'd better get out and search this property for some others who are missing. They may be hidden in a barn or storm cellar. *(threatening again)* And when Ruby gets back, don't you dare tip her off, or you're dead!

Billy: But what about her?

Blanche: *(will full confidence)* We'll take care of Ruby. *(Sol and Mrs. Sloane look at each other in dispair and mouth "How?")* Just do as I say.

Billy: *(obediently)* Yes ma'am. Will you put in a good word fer me with the Feds? *(turning to Sol, quickly)* But tell your son I don't have nothin' personal 'gainst the Mafia. *(back to Blanche)* Will you do it?

Blanche: It all depends on how well you cooperate. I'm not making any promises.

Billy: Anything you say, lady. *(exits, closing door)*

Blanche: Mrs. Sloane, Mr. Finkelstein, you were splendid!

Sol: *(bitten by the acting bug)* You know this acting business isn't too bad. Maybe it's time for a Jewish "Mensch Who Came to Dinner."

Blanche: We'll file that idea for later. *(whips out a hair brush, compact and a long tulle or chiffon scarf. Hurriedly primps and does a theatrical thing with scarf on head while instructing the other two)* Right now, it is Lady McBeth. *(indicating Ruby offstage)* that needs our full attention. Just in case she gets here before Devon does, we'll have to make the best of what we have. We need a plan of attack.

Sol: Act, I can do. Karate, I can't!

Blanche: Sol, you need to be near the door to trip her with your cane. Mrs. Sloane, when she falls, you trap her *(gesturing a strong attack)* with your walker, and – well, we'll improvise from there. *(prepares to use walkie-talkie)*

Ruby: *(offstage right)* Billy, where the hell are you? I told you to come back here and help me! Billy! Do you hear me? *(She kicks the door open; Enters with big cardboard carton, expecting to find Billy)* You lazy SOB, I have to do every – *(sees Blanche standing in command with walkie-talkie)* Holy shit! *(drops carton and turns to excape. The three "captives" carry out Blanche's plan: Sol hooks Ruby's ankle with his cane; as Ruby falls, Mrs. Sloane attacker with her walker, pinning Ruby to the floor. Ruby, stunned, does not fight back.)*

Sol: *(amazed and proud)* I think we did that real good! She's out cold.

Mrs. Sloane: *(worried)* She's not dead is she?

Blanche: I can see her breathing. She was stunned when she met the floor. Let's hope she stays out till Devon gets here. *(on the walkie-talkie)* Devon, the main attraction is out cold on the floor. Sure hope you're ready to move in. Don't know how long we'll – *(interupted by Devon's entrance)*

Devon bursts in followed by a concerned Brent

Brent: *(rushing to Blanche)* Thank God you're alive! Are you alright?

Devon: Of course, she's alright. *(with admiration)* Look at her! She just played the greatest role of her career. *(then tenderly to Blanche)* You are alright, aren't you?

After convincing himself that Blanche and friends are okay, Devon goes about the business of reviving Ruby, whom he handcuffs and brings to her feet during the following two speeches.

Brent: Weren't you frightened?

Blanche: There were a few anxious moments, but I'm old-fashioned enough to believe that the men in my life will come to my rescue. But, Brent, what are you doing here? How did you know about this?

Devon: *(shoving the handcuffed Ruby out the door calls offstage)* Hey, Mack. Here's "the brains". She's all yours! *(turns back to Blanche)* You're lucky you have a friend like this young man. He spotted me – a stranger – hanging around the theatre and was worried – had me checked out, and that led him to the Bureau office.

Blanche: *(kissing Brent)* You're a dear to be so concerned. If only I was thirty years younger, and that's stretching the point a bit. Oh, well. *(to Devon)* What about our fellow victims?

Devon: Good news. There is a barn where they were concealed, and they're a little the worse for wear, but they'll be okay, and they're anxious to testify against Ruby. We're very lucky – thanks to you and your friends.

Blanche: Very dear and talented friends, *(eyeing Mrs. Sloane and Sol kindly)* without whom I never could have succeeded. Devon and Brent, meet Mrs. Sloane and Mr. Finkelstein. *(All shake hands.)*

Devon: *(to Mrs. Sloane)* The Bureau congratulates you for your courage. *(to Sol)* By the way, Mr. Finkelstein, I have a personal message for you – from your son.

Sol: My son? Norman sent me a personal message?

Devon: Yes, he called the home earlier today to speak to you. He wanted to invite you to your grandson's bar mitzvah. He especially wants you there next week.

Sol: *(very moved)* My grandson? Bar mitzvah? Maybe we can work this out after all. *(to Blanche and Mrs. Sloane)* Would you ladies do me the honor of attending the celebration with me?

Blanche: Sol, darling, *(kisses him)* I wouldn't think of missing it.

Mrs. Sloane: I'd be honored, Mrs. Finkelstein. My father's best friend was a rabbi.

Devon: What a proud boy he'll be – showing off his hero grandfather. You'll all be national celebrities after tomorrow's press conference at ten.

Mrs. Sloane: *(fretting)* Ten o'clock? Oh, dear, my best suit is packed and probably all wrinkled, and I need a hairdresser, and –

Devon: *(kindly)* Believe me, you're beautiful as you are, Mrs. Sloane. *(Mrs. Sloane loves this attention.)*

Brent: *(to Blanche)* I insist you go as you are, darling. In that outfit you can announce your latest role in a revival of *(Pajama Game)*. That should shock and astonish the homefolks!

Blanche: Sounds intriguing, but we'll have to postpone it temporarily. I'm signed to run the Boston marathon, remember? I need to get back into training immediately.

Brent: Whatever you say. It'll be worth the wait. We'll keep the star on the dressing room door all shined up – just for you.

Sol: *(to Brent)* Well, it so happens, I'm between engagements. And *(ready to launch a new career)* have I got an idea for you!

Brent: Oh, yes? What is it? *(rolling Sol toward exit door)*

Sol: Have you ever thought of a Jewish "Mensch Who Came To Dinner"? *(reaching the door)* I was just thinking . . . *(Brent and Sol exit as conversation continues)*

Mrs. Sloane: *(in walker, following Brent)* Oh, Brent, dear, wait up! I also have an idea. Have you ever thought of some sort of "booster" organization. Perhaps starting with a nice opening night gala. *(exits)*

Devon: Well, Blanche, you're one gutsy lady.

Blanche: It's easy to be gutsy when a knight in shining armour is ready with the rescue. We say in the theatre that timing is everything.

Devon: No way I would have missed your final big scene.

Blanche: *(happily)* Wasn't bad. A Happy Ending and a Fast Curtain.

BLACKOUT

All the Comforts of Home

by Howard T. Amend

All the Comforts of Home

by Howard T. Amend

Cast List

Gracie	Endora	Narrator
Miranda	Cletus	
Sara	Ambrose	

All the Comforts of Home

by Howard T. Amend

SCENE ONE

The entire action of the play takes place in the combination front-room – dining room of Miranda's home. Time: The Present.

At Rise: It is about 9 a.m. and Miranda and Sara are sitting at the dining table, front and center, enjoying their morning coffee. Gracie enters from the kitchen door at left. She is carrying a tray.

Gracie: Here's some fresh cinnamon rolls – right from the oven.

Miranda: Thank you, Gracie.

Sara: They look delicious!

Gracie: Is the morning paper here yet?

Miranda: No! Gracie, honey, will you be a dear and get it for me?

Gracie: Certainly, Miranda! *(she exits at right.)*

Sara: *(to Miranda)* Do you think our classified ad will be in today's paper?

Miranda: It certainly should be! They promised me faithfully that it would be in today's classified section.

Gracie: *(enters from the right. She pauses a moment and reads aloud.)* Counterfeiter active in local area. Middle aged man suspected of passing bogus bills – Law enforcement agencies are hopeful of an early arrest. Oh! Here Miranda.

Miranda: Thank you dear! *(She eagerly takes paper and turns the pages.)*

Gracie: How did you like the rolls, Sara?

Sara: Delightfully delectable!

Miranda: *(trimuphantly)* Ah! Here we are!

Gracie: Read it aloud, please.

Miranda: *(clears throat)* "Tenants, anyone? Share my home and expenses with three congenial ladies — No smoke — No pets, 6800 W. Westshore Court – 679-0530."

Sara: *(proudly)* Wrote it myself! Should bring results! *(phone rings noisily)*

73

Miranda: *(answers)* Hello! Yes! I'm the lady who placed the ad. What's that? Do we smoke pot? Oh – we burn the oatmeal once in awhile. What's that? Smoke grass? No! We place the grass clippings in the compost heap. What? Honey, may I ask you your age? Nineteen? How old are we? Well, I'm 73 – Gracie is 71 and Sara is 68! Hello? Hello? Why she hung up on me! The little snip!

Sara: She seemed to have a lot of hang-ups!

Gracie: Share experiences with us? She must be desperate!*(sound of door chimes)*

Gracie: I'll get it!

Miranda: Another answer to my ad!

Sara: *(to herself)* Our ad!

Gracie: Miranda, here is a lady about the ad in the paper.

Endora: *(enters from right and says pontifically)* I am Mrs. Endora Westbrook. I read your advertisement in this morning's paper. *(she peers disdainfully through her lorgnette)* Is this it?

Mirana: Yes, my dear, this is it!

Endora: May I ask what happened to the previous tenant?

Miranda: Ah--a! Well, Phoebe was our beloved and trusted friend. We all loved her dearly and treasured her cordiality so very much. But one day she suddenly left us . . .

Endora: She moved out?

Sara: She died.

Endora: *(cringes at the word)* Merciful heavens! She died? Tell me – was it contagious?

Sara: She had a heart attack.

Gracie: The poor dear!

Sara: Heart attacks are not contagious.

Endora: Humph! I suppose you have maid service?

Mirana: No! You will have to take care of your own room.

Endora: Take care of my own room? I am a Westbrook! I never made a bed in my life, I'll have you know!

Miranda: And we all share the household chores. Cooking, cleaning, dishwashing, etc.

Endora: Oh, no! Tell me – how is the cuisine?

Miranda: Well, tonight we're having corned beef and cabbage, boiled potatoes, stewed carrots, parkerhouse rolls and apple pie and coffee.

Endora: What mundane fare! No filet mignon or poached salmon? I think I'm going to be ill.

Gracie: You look ill!

Sara: *(dryly)* She's hungry!

Endora: Tell me. Do you have a tennis court?

Gracie: We have a ping-pong table in the basement.

Sara: *(hopefully)* Do you play pinocle?

Endora: You poor peasants! No tennis – no bridge! Tell me – do you have a sauna?

Miranda: We share the bathroom.

Endora: Only one bathtub – isn't that terribly unsanitary?

Gracie: We wash it out when we're finished.

Sara: That phrase has a familiar ring to it!

Endora: *(sarcastically)* How much a month for all this luxury?

Miranda: Two hundred and seventy five dollars a month. In advance.

Endora: In advance? Merciful heaven! I'm afraid that this place is definitely not for me. I must bid you adieu. *(She turns to leave and Gracie escorts her to the door at right.)*

Gracie: *(to Endora)* Goodbye, dear! Oh, yes! The Waldorf Plaza is six blocks down the street.

Miranda: Did you notice that ratty old mink stole she was wearing? No doubt that it has seen better days.

Sara: And that lorgnette has obviously seen better times.

Gracie: Poor dear. *(the phone rings noisily and Gracie answers)* Hello? You don't say! *(pause)* You don't say . . . you don't say . . . you don't say! *(She hangs up receiver.)*

Miranda and Sara: *(in unison)* Who was it?

Gracie: I don't know! They didn't say! *(the phone rings again)*

Miranda: Ah – ah! Never mind, Gracie – I'll answer it! *(she picks up phone)* Hello? Oh! You've read our advertisement? You like the arrangement? Fine! How much? Two hundred and seventy five dollars a month. No problem? Fine! Why don't you come out and see our home? Oh! Oh! You have a pet? I'm sorry, lady! We do not allow pets. What kind of a pet do you have? *(incredulously)* A boa constrictor? Oh, my! Oh, my! And it feeds on live mice? Mice? Oh, dear!

Gracie: I think I'm going to faint!

Sara: Hickory-dickory-dock! A mouse ran up my sock! That's all we need – live mice!

Miranda: I'm very sorry, my dear, but the other ladies here – and myself have an aversion to reptiles and mice. No reflection on you though. I understand. You cannot part with your pet . . .

Sara: It's probably wrapped around her . . . she can't part with it!

Gracie: Or vice-versa!

Miranda: Very well, thank you for calling. Goodbye! *(hangs up)* *(Sound of door bell chimes)*

Gracie: I'll get it! *(she walks briskly to the front door)*

Miranda: It's a man, Miranda!

Sara: A man? This might be my lucky day!

Miranda: Tell him to come in.

Sara: By all means!

Gracie: This is Mr. Cletus Culpepper.

Miranda: *(affably)* Good morning, Mr. Culpepper, what can we do for you?

Cletus: I'm here in answer to your ad in this morning's paper. *(He has copy of paper in his hand)*

Miranda: Mr. Culpepper, there must be some mistake! Our ad clearly states that we desired a female tenant.

Cletus: Not necessarily. If you permit me to say so. *(He reads ad)* "Share My Home and Expenses with three congenial ladies." *(puts down paper)* Obviously, you three ladies are congenial – I can see that! I'm interested in sharing your home!

Miranda: But . . . but Mr. Culpepper . . .

Cletus: *(patiently)* Call me Cletus!

Miranda: But Mr. Culpepper – ah, Cletus! You are a man!

Cletus: Yes. That's right!

Sara: Quite right!

Miranda: Mr. Culpepper –

Cletus: *(gently)* Cletus!

Miranda: Cletus! It just won't work out! What will the neighbors think? What about the bathroom? We only have one, you know!

Cletus: My dear lady, don't worry about the neighbors and don't worry about the bathroom! As an old married man who had two daughters. I am quite used to lingerie and panty hose hanging in the bathroom.

Sara: Where is your wife?

Cletus: I'm a widower, ma'am.

Sara: Oh! I'm sorry!

Miranda: It just won't work out, I'm afraid! There is the moral aspect to consider . . . one man and three unattached ladies . . . *(shakes her head)*

Cletus: Our arrangement will be purely platonic, I assure you. You will not have to worry about me walking in my sleep . . . and don't worry about morals . . . in my case, the golden days are over.

Gracie: What's he trying to tell us?

Sara: He's impotent!

Gracie: Important?

Sara: No! Impotent!

Gracie: Impotent – important! What's the difference?

Sara: Honey, there's a whale of a lot of difference!

Miranda: But, Cletus! You will have to take care to your own room and we all share in the household chores. We take turns cooking.

Sara: Can you cook?

Cletus: That is one of my hobbies.

Miranda: If today was your turn in the kitchen what would be on the menu?

Cletus: *(without hesitation)* Breakfast: Buckwheat pancakes, bacon, applesauce, coffee or milk. Lunch: A bowl of vegetable soup, grilled cheese sandwiches, tea or Kool-aid. Dinner: Meat loaf, baked potatoes, spinach, avocado salad, chocolate pudding for dessert, tea or coffee.

Miranda: Say! That sounds good!

Sara: I'm getting a little weary of our cuisine!

Gracie: Yes! We have too many Indians and not enough chefs!

Miranda: It's all very nice but it will just never work!

Cletus: You'll have to admit – it would be nice to have a man round the house – to fix that leaky faucet, a running toilet, paint the front porch, repair an electrical switch, mow the lawn . . .

Miranda: Stop, Cletus! Please stop!

Gracie: The lamp in my room doesn't work.

Sara: The little light in the frigidaire doesn't burn anymore!

Cletus: There! You see? Another fringe benefit – I have a 1980 Datsun station wagon. I could take you shopping or we could go on a picnic or for a ride to the beach. *(Or some local resort)*

Gracie: The last ride I had was in the limousine when they laid poor Phoebe away!

Miranda: Believe me, Cletus, you tempt us. But we ladies will have to take a vote. We do things the democratic way around here. Cletus, dear, why don't you take a look at your room? It's upstairs, the first door to the left.

Cletus: Very well – thank you! *(He exits left)*

Miranda: Well, ladies! You have heard all the evidence, do I hear a motion that we rent the room to Cletus . . . I mean . . . Mr. Culpepper?

Gracie: I make the motion that we rent the room to Cletus!

Sara: Second the motion!

Miranda: The motion has been seconded. We will now have the vote.

Gracie: Aye!

Sara: We know so very little about this man. He could be Jack the Ripper or an axe murderer for all we know. But I like his eyes and I love his cologne! I vote aye!

Miranda: He's no Robert Redford. But he is nearly dressed and did you notice his clean finger nails? I vote aye! The motion is carried.

Cletus: *(enters from the left)* Ladies, the room is just beautiful – you have such a charming home!

Miranda: The rent is two hundred and seventy five dollars in advance.

Cletus: That's fine. *(chuckles to himself)* Money is no problem with me. If you will permit me to use your garage for my car and if you will allow me a corner in your basement for my small off-set press I will pay you an additional twenty five dollars a month. How does that sound to you?

Miranda: I'll go along with that!

Gracie: What do you use a set-off press for, Cletus?

Cletus: *(smiles)* An off-set press, my dear. I do a little moonlighting – printing business cards, letter-heads, fliers, etc.

Miranda: Make your check out to me – Miranda Winthrop.

Cletus: Very good. *(writes out check)* Now, if I may see the basement for a moment?

Miranda: Surely. Go through the kitchen, on the left, and go down the stairs. We do have a nice basement.

Cletus: Fine. Ladies, if you will excuse me? *(he exits at 1st door on left; Sound of door chimes)*

Gracie: I'll get it! *(she answers door and returns)* It's a man!

Miranda: Another man? Tell him that the room has been rented. Oh, well. Show him in.

Gracie: *(returns with a man)* This is Mr. Armstrong, we just rented it.

Ambrose: *(smiles)* I'm not looking for a room, my dear lady, I'm looking for a man!

Sara: You too?

Ambrose: My name is Ambrose Armstrong, I am an agent for the U.S. Treasury Department. Here are my credentials. Tell me, is that your 1980 Datsun station wagon with the chromium luggage rack out there in your driveway?

Miranda: Heavens, no! I don't own a car. That's Mr. Culpepper's auto.

Ambrose: And, my I ask where Mr. Culpepper is now?

Gracie: He's in the basement. He's going to set up his set-up press.

Sara: Offset press.

Ambrose: Ah, yes! Mr. Culpepper is a printer, I take it?

Mianda: Yes! He prints business cards, letter-heads, fliers, etc.

Ambrose: Among other things! I would like to meet your Mr. Culpepper.

Miranda: Well, here he is now. (*Cletus has returned from the basement enters from left.*)

Cletus: Oh! I see you have company! I can leave by the back door!

Ambrose: Just a moment, Mr. Culpepper, I would like to have a word with you! Are you Cletus Culpepper, formerly of 1883 Rockwood Avenue, of this city?

Cletus: Oh, oh! The jig is up, huh?

Ambrose: I'm afraid it is, Culpepper! I am Ambrose Armstrong from the U. S. Treasury Department – here are my credentials! You are under arrest! You have the right to remain silent, you . . .

Cletus: Skip the rights, Ambrose! I'll go quietly! (*holds out his hands*)

Miranda: (*aghast*) What will the neighbors think?

Gracie: There goes our ride to the beach!

Sara: That light in the frigidaire will never be fixed now!

Ambrose: (*puts the handcuffs on Cletus*) Thank you, Culpepper, for your cooperation.

Miranda: May I ask why you are arresting Cletus . . . oh, I mean Mr. Culpepper?

Ambrose: Mr. Culpepper is an alleged counterfeiter. We have been looking for him for a long time.

Gracie: (*to Sara*) I don't understand. Did he make confederate money or counterfeit money?

Sara: Counterfeit money!

Gracie: Confederate money – counterfeit money – what's the difference?

Sara: Honey, there's a whale of a lot of difference!

Ambrose: Very aptly put ma'am!

Cletus: Tell me, Ambrose, I'm curious. How did you find me out?

Ambrose: It was the chromium luggage rack on your station wagon that proved to be your undoing.

Cletus: (*incredulously*) What? What did a chromium luggage rack have to do with my arrest?

Ambrose: You passed a bogus ten dollar bill at a cleaning establishment about a week ago.

Cletus: *(puzzled)* Yes! But I still don't see . . .

Ambrose: The attendant had solvent on her hands and some of the green ink rubbed off on her fingers. She spotted you getting into a 1980 Datsun station wagon with a chromium rack on the top. She failed to get your license number but she did give us a good description of you and the car. The rest was leg work.

Cletus: That confounded luggage rack was my Achilles heel!

Ambrose: We ran all the 1980 Datsun station wagon owners through the computer and your name popped out. We then ran all the names and descriptions of all the lithographers in this area and presto – your name again! We closed in on your last address but you had just left.

Cletus: I thought that the ink was perfect!

Ambrose: Tell me, I'm curious. Why did you print ten dollar bills? Most counterfeiters prefer to print twenties.

Cletus: I know! That's why I decided to make tens. Everyone is suspicious of a new twenty but they accept a ten-spot without question. They wouldn't notice if Alexander Hamilton was cross-eyed.

Ambrose: You were very ingenious, Culpepper, I must say. Your plates were well-nigh perfect. But your paper was outstanding – you even duplicated the watermark.

Cletus: *(proudly)* I designed a little machine similar to an agate tumbler to give the bills a weathered look. I folded some and crumpled others and soiled a few with a little dirt or grease.

Ambrose: Ingenious!

Cletus: But it was tiresome hustling around changing my funny money for the real stuff. I only deposited genuine money in my checking account at my bank.

Ambrose: As far as we could determine, you never had a confederate and you never sold your money to syndicate at a discount.

Cletus: That's right! I was never greedy. I never got rich. I just used the dough to pay expenses.

Ambrose: May I ask what it was that induced you to make counterfeit money?

Cletus: Before I was retired, my wife had an extended illness and the medical bills were staggering as our health insurance was inadequate. But printing bogus money was wrong and I have no excuses. I am guilty – I broke the law and deserve the punishment. I'll take my lumps.

Ambrose: I am sorry, Culpepper. If you will tell me where the plates are we will be on our way!

Cletus: Surely. They're in the spare tire well in the trunk of my car.

Ambrose: Goodbye, ladies! Thank you for your cooperation. I will send a man to pick up Mr. Culpepper's printing paraphernalia and car. They will be impounded.

Cletus: *(bows gallantly)* Goodbye, dear ladies! I apologize for the embarrassment and confusion I have caused you.

Miranda: *(tearfully)* It's been nice knowing you, Cletus. Here, I'm returning your three hundred dollar check.

Cletus: You may keep it, dear lady!

Miranda: No! *(she tears up check)*

Gracie: *(to Cletus with emotion)* When will you come back

Sara: *(hopefully)* Maybe you can print license plates.

Cletus: *(smiles)* Yes! Sounds like fun! Goodbye, ladies! *(Cletus and Ambrose exit at right. There is a pause . . . the three women are mulling over the events of the past hour.)*

Miranda: This has been an exhausting morning. I'm going upstairs and take a little nap.

Sara: And I'm going to the kitchen and make a meat loaf. We are going to have baked potatoes, spinach, avocado salad and chocolate pudding for supper. Watch the phone, Gracie! Call me if you need me.

Gracie: Okay! *(Sara exits to the kitchen on left. Gracie adjusts her body to the chair and her eyes close. She has a serene expression on her face – her head drops once . . . twice . . . and she is fast asleep. After a short pause, the narrator enters from the right – she stands near the footlights and puts her forefinger to her lips for silence. She looks at her wrist watch and then nods toward the sleeping Gracie and says:)*

Narrator: Two hours have passed while Gracie has been sleeping and evidently Miranda is still upstairs while Sara is busily engaged in preparing supper. *(She sniffs appreciatively)* H-m-m-n! Meat loaf! I hear someone on the porch! *(She puts her finger to her lips again . . . smiles . . . and exits at right . . . sound of door chimes . . . pause – chimes ring again . . . just as Gracie is awakening, Sara enters from kitchen at left.)*

Sara: Gracie! Honey! The door bell!

Miranda: *(from off stage) (with some irritation)* Will somebody answer the door?

Gracie: *(apologetically)* Oh! I was just resting my eyes! Oh! The door! I'll get it! *(She gets up from her chair and scurries to the front door. Miranda and Sara enter from left front and left rear – simultaneously. They work toward the table and look curiously at the front door)*

Gracie: Well! Hello! *(excitedly)* Why it's you! It's you! Come in! Come in!

Miranda: Who is it Gracie?

Gracie: *(enters and says gleefully)* Look! Ladies! It's Cletus! *(exuberantly)* He's back! He's back!

Miranda: Cletus! This is a pleasure! It's so good to see you again! We thought that you were in the . . .

Sara: . . . the slammer . . . the pokey!

Cletus: *(happily)* Hello, dear ladies! It's good to see you again! It's great to be out!

Gracie: You remind me so much of James Cagney! You didn't break out, did you?

Cletus: *(laughs)* Break out? Heavens, no!

Sara: But you are out!

Cletus: I'm out on bail. I was released on my own recognizance. My lawyer says that it may be months before my case comes to trial.

Miranda: That's wonderful! I mean . . . at least – you are out!

Sara: What are your present plans?

Cletus: I came back to pick up my car. The Treasury Department will confiscate my press.

Miranda: But what are your plans, Cletus? Where will you stay?

Cletus: Well, the first thing I will have to do is find a room . . .

Miranda: Cletus! You are welcome to stay here – at least until your . . .

Sara: . . . trial comes up!

Cletus: That's just great! Are you sure that you don't mind? I just don't know what to say. This morning I did not know you ladies and now you are very much concerned about my welfare . . . I just . . . well, I think that I have something in my eye!

Gracie: We'd love to have you!

Sara: Yes! We have dinner at 4:30. Meat loaf, baked potatoes, spinach, avocado salad, tea or coffee. For dessert I baked an up-side-down cake.

Gracie: I just love down-side-up cakes! You put the frosting on the bottom and the raisins and walnuts on top. It's not so messy that way!

Cletus: *(finishes writing a check and hands it to Miranda)* I'm very grateful, ladies. I'll go out and get my suitcase and then I'll repair Gracie's lamp and replace the light in the frigidaire. Then I'll replace that loose step on the porch.

Miranda: Oh! Cletus! We would be forever grateful!

Cletus: And tomorrow we'll take a little ride to the coast! How does that sound to you ladies?

Miranda: *(fervently)* It's so nice to have a man around the house!

Sara: *(emphatically)* You can say that again!

Gracie: *(with enthusiasum)* It's so nice to have a man around the house!

CURTAIN

The Lalapalooza Bird
by Tim Kelly

The Lalapalooza Bird

by Tim Kelly

Cast List

Grandpa	Sarah
Ginny	Ralph
Estelle	Mrs. Baker

The Lalapalooza Bird

by Tim Kelly

Setting: The porch of a beach shanty. Anything that adds to the "seaside effect" is helpful – fishnet, shells, fishing gear, etc. However, the essential properties are few. They are a weather-beaten rocking chair and a slightly battered chair, with a small table in between, at Right. A wooden bench is off to the side, Left. Entrance into the shanty is Up Right. Entrances to the porch from the beach are Down Right and Down Left.

At rise: We hear the voice of Grandpa Todd from inside the shanty, singing:

Grandpa: "Fifteen men on a dead man's chest, Yo, ho, ho, and a bottle of rum!" *(In a moment he appears carrying a tray. On the tray is a pitcher of lemonade and two glasses. He sets the tray on the table, recites with gusto.)*
   "Our captain stood upon the deck,
     A spy-glass in his hand,
    A-viewing of those gallant whales
     That blew at every strand."

(He stands straight, makes a fist with each hand, puts them together to suggest a "telescope" and puts them to his eye. He scans the horizon) Not a whale in sight. *(Sighs)* Pity. *(Grandpa Todd is a strong-looking man who obviously enjoys the outdoors. He is intelligent and friendly with a love and appreciation of life that's genuine. He wears a pair of faded dungarees, a work shirt, and a "skipper" or "sailor" hat)*

Ginny: *(From offstage Left)* Mr. Todd! Mr. Todd!

Grandpa: *(Puts down his "telescope," calls Down Left)* Over here, Ginny. On the porch. *(He works the "telescope" again, Ginny, an appealing girl, about 12, a shade on the tomboy side, enters Down Left. She carries a pail)*

Ginny: Mrs. Baker sent you some clams. Said you shouldn't be afraid of them. Said you'd enjoy them. Said to wash them good. Said –

Grandpa: *(Cuts in)* Mrs. Baker does say a lot, doesn't she?

Ginny: She likes to talk, if that's what you mean.

Grandpa: *(Laughs)* Tell her I'm much obliged for the clams. Just set them on the bench. *(Ginny puts the pail on the bench, observes Grandpa with his "telescope")*

Ginny: Looking for whales again?

Grandpa: Yep. I'm searching the horizon.

Ginny: What's that?

Grandpa: Horizon?

Ginny: Unh-hunh.

Grandpa: It's where the sky and the earth appear to meet. See? Out across the water. It's almost a straight line.

Ginny: I've seen that before. Only I didn't know it was the, uh, uh –

Grandpa: Horizon.

Ginny: Horizon.

Grandpa: Right. Pour yourself some lemonade, Ginny. (*Ginny steps to the table, pours herself a glass, drinks as they converse*)

Ginny: (*As Grandpa does "telescope" business again*) Wouldn't a real telescope work better?

Grandpa: Anyone can use a real telescope, Ginny. I prefer this one. It helps the imagination.

Ginny: (*Sits on bench*) Doesn't cost as much as a real one either.

Grandpa: You're much too young to be so practical, Ginny.

Ginny: (*Old beyond her years*) I suppose I am. No one ever sees a whale in these parts, Mr. Todd.

Grandpa: That's why imagination is so important. (*Recites*) Maybe we didn't see a whale yesterday and maybe we won't see a whale today, but that doesn't mean we won't see one tomorrow. (*Scanning the horizon*) Just one span – one great span.

Ginny: Hunh?

Grandpa: Span.

Ginny: Is that anything like a "horizon"?

Grandpa: Not in the least. (*Lowers "telescope" again*) A span is the distance from one rise of the whale to the other.

Ginny: You sure know a bucketful about the ocean. You were a sailor, I bet.

Grandpa: No, Ginny. I worked in an office. They only sailing I did was between filing cabinets. Always wanted to be a man of the sea, though.

Ginny: If you wanted to be a sailing man, why did you work in an office?

Grandpa: We can't always do what we'd like.

Ginny: Why not?

Grandpa: Life.

Ginny: (*Doesn't understand*) Hunh?

Grandpa: Didn't you ever want something you couldn't have?

Ginny: You mean – like parents? *(Grandpa looks at her; there is a moment of awkward silence. Ginny hops up)* I better see what Ralph's up to. He gets into trouble when I'm not around.

Grandpa: I've got some chores inside. You take your time and finish your lemonade. Ralph can wait. Don't gulp.

He goes into the shanty. Ginny puts down her glass, stands, and makes a "telescope" with her fists, scans. Estelle, Grandpa Todd's daughter, enters Down Right. She is looking at a slip of paper she holds in her hand. She's in her 30's or 40's, intelligent but rather prim

Estelle: Excuse me, young lady.

Ginny: Hunh? *(Lowers "telescope")*

Estelle: I'm looking for Windward Cottage.

Ginny: This is it.

Estelle: *(Appalled)* This?

Ginny: Unh-hunh.

Estelle: There must be some mistake. *(Checks paper)* Perhaps I have the wrong address.

Ginny: There's only one Windward Cottage on this beach.

Estelle: It's not a cottage at all. Its – *(searches for the right word)* – a shanty.

Ginny: Yup. Most of the cottages along the waterline are shanties. Folks only use them in the summertime. Except for Mrs. Baker. She's got a "year-round." Betcha don't know what I'm doing. *("telescope" again)* I'm scanning the horizon for whales.

Estelle: I'm looking for Mister Todd.

Ginny: Hey, Mr. Todd! Company. *(To Estelle)* I better check out my brother. He needs me to look out for him. *(Ginny darts off, Down Left. Estelle steps onto the porch, apprehensive. She looks at the worn furniture as if she suspected it might change shape if she stared hard enough. Grandpa enters from the shanty)*

Grandpa: Who is it, Ginny?

Estelle: *(Forces a smile)* Hello, Dad.

Grandpa: Estelle? Why didn't you tell me you were coming down?

Estelle: I wanted it to be a surprise.

Grandpa: *(Grins wide)* Welcome. *(He embraces her. She kisses him dutifully on the cheek)* Sit down, sit down. *(He gestures to chair Left. She sits)* You're in luck.

Estelle: Oh?

Grandpa: The lemonade. I just made it. Fresh.

Estelle: No, thanks. I stopped and had lunch. Such a lovely day and the restaurant had a terrace overlooking the water.

Grandpa: I'll pour myself a glass.

Estelle: Yes, do. *(Both are trying to be pleasant and noncomittal, but the attempt is one of evasion. They are trying to avoid a "certain" subject, but each knows this will not be possible)* Who was the girl here on the porch?

Grandpa: Ginny. Lives with Mrs. Baker. She takes children in. *(He sits in the rocker with his lemonade)*

Estelle: What do you mean she takes them in?

Grandpa: They have no place to go. Some are battered children, some are runaways that won't go home, some have no homes to go to, and some are simply unloved. Unwanted.

Estelle: She must have a big heart.

Grandpa: And a big house. That helps. *(Indicates pail)* She sent Ginny with a pail of clams.

Estelle: *(Stands, nervous)* You can't be comfortable here.

Grandpa: You haven't even seen the inside, Estelle.

Estelle: This place is nothing but a shack.

Grandpa: It's only for the summer.

Estelle: Then what?

Grandpa: *(Evasively)* We'll see.

Estelle: That's another way of saying you have no intention of returning. You have a perfectly good room of your own in our apartment.

Grandpa: Estelle, I know this is difficult for you, but I'd rather live in this "shack," as you call it, than in that room you fixed up for me.

Estelle: That's cruel.

Grandpa: Let me finish, darlin', and it's not cruel. You and Thomas have your own lives. It's not as if I was incapable of caring for myself. *(Wistful)* After your mother died I admit I was in something of a state, not myself at all. I'll always be grateful for the love and concern you and your husband showed me, but, now, I've got to get on with this business of living. Living my life.

Estelle: *(Beginning to break with frustration)* I can't let my own father live in squalor like this – I won't accept it.

Grandpa: You must.

Estelle: No!

Grandpa: I am not coming back to the apartment.

Estelle: *(Tense)* If you don't I'll never forgive myself! I'll never forgive you. I mean that.

Grandpa: Stop it.

Estelle: No – never!

Sarah, Estelle's daughter, about 11 or 12, enters Down Right. Estelle sees her coming and turns away to hide her tears. Grandpa is delighted to see Sarah

Sarah: Hello, Grandpa.

Grandpa: There she is! There's my Sarah! Best li'l granddaughter in the whole wide world! *(He hunkers, throws open his arms. Sarah rushes to him. They embrace. Sarah is a bright girl, precocious)*

Sarah: I wanted to telephone. Mother said it would be more of a surprise this way.

Grandpa: Sit down and have some lemonade. I better get some more ice. Melts in this weather. *(He picks up pitcher, gives a concerned glance to Estelle, exits)*

Sarah: *(She sits in the rocker)* I wish we lived on the beach.

Estelle: You wouldn't like it in the winter.

Sarah: Why not?

Estelle: It's bitterly cold and none of these shacks have decent heating.

Sarah: Where will Grandpa live in the winter?

Estelle: He'll be back with us in the apartment. Where he belongs. *(Estelle steps to the "door" of the shanty, checks to see that Grandpa can't hear, steps to Sarah and speaks with the tone of a conspirator)* Sarah, you're a bright girl, so I know I can count on you. We can't abandon him. I could ask him to come back again and again and he wouldn't. He's stubborn. Your father could plead and it wouldn't do much good, either. *(Pause)* So it's up to you, Sarah.

Sarah: What is?

Estelle: Tell him how much you miss him.

Sarah: He already knows that. He knows I miss him more than anything.

Estelle: Then persuading him to come home won't be too difficult. *(Hopeful)* Will it?

Sarah: I don't want him to do anything he doesn't want to do.

Estelle: *(Irritated)* You haven't been listening. Your grandfather doesn't know what he wants. You've got to make him see that he doesn't belong in this place. He –

Grandpa: *(From inside)*
"Oh, Shenandoah, I long to hear you
    Away you rolling river,
Oh, Shenandoah, I long to hear you
    Way a-way, I'm bound a-way
'Cross the wide Missouri . . . "
(During song, Estelle crosses Down Right)

Sarah: Where are you going?

Estelle: *(Nervously)* I'll take a stroll along the beach. I'm counting on you, Sarah. *(Estelle hurriedly exits. Sarah stands. Still singing. Grandpa enters from shanty. Sarah moves behind table)*

Sarah: You still like to sing, Grandpa.

Grandpa: That's a fact. Can't deny it. I forgot to fill up the tray. No more ice for a while, I'm afraid.

Sarah: *(Pouring a glass of lemonade)* I'll use my imagination – like you taught me. *(Pointedly)* We have an ice-maker at home. All the ice anyone could want.

Grandpa: *(Fixes her with a critical eye)* Hmmmm. If I didn't know better I'd swear that was Estelle talking. *(Looks about)* Where's your mother?

Sarah: She wanted to take a walk along the beach.

Grandpa: *(Suspicious)* Oh?

Sarah: Maybe she wants to collect some shells.

Grandpa: Your mother doesn't like shells in the house. You know that. They scratch the woodwork.

Sarah: Maybe she wants to take off her shoes and get her feet wet.

Grandpa: Maybe she wanted you to persuade me to come back to the apartment. *(They look at each other for a moment and then break out into wide grins)*

Sarah: I knew I couldn't fool you.

Grandpa: *(Sits Right)* I do miss you, Sarah.

Sarah: I miss you, too, Grandpa. I wanted to come see you sooner, but Mother was so upset about you leaving that she didn't want to hear about the beach.

Grandpa: Estelle is a wonderful woman, but she does want to live other people's lives. Living her own life ought to be a full-time job. *(Sarah steps behind the rocker and puts her arms around her Grandfather, hugs)* Your mother and father should be able to do what they want without worrying about me.

Sarah: And you should be able to do what you want without worrying about them?

Grandpa: Couldn't have said it better myself. Doesn't mean we've stopped loving each other, or needing each other, or helping each other.

Sarah: Then what does it mean?

Grandpa: That every human being needs a little dignity. Some independence. That's very precious.

Sarah: Dad said you can't afford to be independent.

Grandpa: You'd be surprised how easy it is to get by with a little independence and a few friends. Like Mrs. Baker.

Sarah: Who's Mrs. Baker?

Grandpa: *(Points to pail)* Today, Mrs. Baker is the "clam lady."

Sarah: Clam lady? *(She crosses to pail, investigates)* Clams. Yeech.

Ralph: *(From offstage Down Left)* Hey, G. T.! G. T.!

Sarah: Who's that?

Grandpa: That's Ralph.

Sarah: What's he shouting?

Grandpa: G. T.

Sarah: What's that?

Grandpa: Short for "Grandpa Todd." Ralph's inventive.

Sarah: He shouldn't call you G. T. It's not respectful.

Grandpa: Don't be smug, Sarah.

(Ralph enters Down Left. He's about Ginny's age. Fast-talking, pretends to be streetwise. Insecure. Despite the warmness of the day he wears a leather jacket dripping with medals, buttons, pins. He wears surfing shorts, is barefooted. In one hand he carries a fishing pole. In the other a rolled up "blueprint")

Ralph: Important business. Gotta talk with you, G. T. *(Notices Sarah)* Who's she?

Grandpa: Ralph, I'd like you to meet my granddaughter. This is Sarah.

Ralph: *(The "Big Shot")* Any granddaughter of G. T.'s is a granddaughter of mine.

Sarah: That's not an intelligent thing to say.

Grandpa: Sarah, your manners.

Sarah: How can I be his granddaughter? I'm probably older than he is. Aren't you hot in that old leather jacket?

Ralph: Naw.

Sarah: Why do you wear it on a day like this?

Ralph: Because I belong to a gang, see. *(Tough)* We never take off our leather. It's a badge of honor.

Sarah: You must take it off when you sleep.

Ralph: I always sleep in my leather.

Sarah: Phew!

Ralph: *(Strides to the table, hands Sarah the fishing pole)* Hold this.

Sarah: Why should I? *(But she takes it. Ralph ignores her, spreads out the "Blueprint")*

Ralph: Tell me what you think, G. T. *(Grandpa looks, Sarah steps closer for a look)*

Grandpa: Hmmm. Unusual. *(Moves a finger over "blueprint")* Has possibilities. *(Rubs his chin, thoughtful)* One question.

Ralph: Any question of yours is a question of mine, G. T. shoot.

Grandpa: What is it?

Ralph: It's a blueprint.

Sarah: That's not a blueprint. It's nothing but some wrapping paper with some crazy lines you've drawn in crayon.

Grandpa: I told you Ralph was inventive. If he says it's a blueprint, it's a blueprint. *(Sarah is not convinced. Ralph is irritated that his "invention" hasn't been recognized at once)*

Ralph: It's a plan for an underwater restaurant!

Grandpa: Mighty clever.

Sarah: How could you breathe?

Ralph: People would sit under the water and breathe pure oxygen while they et.

Sarah: While they what?

Ralph: Et, et. Don't you know what "et" means?

Sarah: I think you mean people would sit under the water and breathe pure oxygen while they ate.

Ralph: I just said that.

Sarah: No you didn't. You said "et." That's not a word. Not even in the dictionary.

Grandpa: I need my glasses for this blueprint.

Ralph: Want me to go and look for them, G. T.?

Sarah: I'll go and look for them. He's _my_ grandfather.

Grandpa: I can find them myself. You two simmer down. Too nice a day for any quarrels. *(Grandpa exits. Sarah sits in the rocker.)*

Ralph: I'm going to make a million by the time I'm sixteen. I've got smarts. I'm tough, too. Anybody who messes with me is going to find himself in trouble. *(Boasts)* I can take care of myself.

Sarah: So can I, but I don't have to wear a leather jacket to prove it.

Ralph: I bet I can spray-can the side of the garage faster than you.

Sarah: Why would I want to do something dumb like that?

Ralph: If you don't spray your name on the side of a garage, how is anyone going to know you're around?

Sarah: My grandfather knows you're around and you didn't spray-can the side of his cottage.

Ralph: *(Sits Left)* I don't do that no more. Kid stuff. I invent things now. My last father showed me how.

Sarah: Your last father? How many do you have?

Ralph: I dunno. Lost count. If things work out maybe Mrs. Baker will be able to keep me. My last father's wife didn't like me too much. Said I was rough in the house. So the social worker had to move me out. I miss my last father, though. He got me started on this underwater restaurant idea.

Sarah: Where's your real father? *(Ralph ignores the question. His method of defense is quite simple. He doesn't "hear" what he doesn't wish to hear)*

Ralph: Betcha I'll make two million dollars. You're lucky to have a grandfather like G. T. Showed me how to work a crossword puzzle and he lets me borrow his books. *(Shrugs)* I don't read so good, though. Sometimes we watch for whales together. He's got this thing for whales. Any day now, I'll get a new father or mother and I bet I'll never get to see a whale.

Sarah: What happened to your gang?

Ralph: What gang? *(Remembers)* Oh, them. *(Boats)* Kid stuff. I don't need a gang no more. I don't need no one. *(Ginny appears Down Left, somewhat agitated)*

Ginny: Where have you been, Ralph? *(Motherly)* You get in trouble when I'm not around. *(Ralph sticks his tongue out between his lips, makes a raspberry. Ginny makes herself right at home, steps onto porch. To Sarah)* My brother is the biggest pain in this town. No wonder he can't make friends.

Ralph: I can make friends. I can make friends faster than anybody.

Sarah: My name's Sarah.

Ralph: *(To Ginny)* She belongs to G. T.

Ginny: *(Sees pail)* The clams! Out in the hot sun! Oh, my goodness! I better take them inside. Oh, my goodness.

Ralph: I ain't stopping you. *(Ginny picks up the pail, exits into shanty.)*

Sarah: I guess your sister didn't want to meet me. Didn't even say hello.

Ralph: She's not my real sister. She was at Mrs. Baker's when I got there. She tells everybody I'm her real brother, but I ain't. *(Corrects himself)* I mean, I'm not.

Sarah: I wonder why she does that?

Ralph: Makes her feel like she got somebody, I guess. I take the place of a teddy bear, ha, ha. I don't pay her no 'tension. I got my inventions.

Sarah: Let me have another look. *(Sarah leans to the table, but Ralph hastily snatches up the "blueprint")*

Ralph: No!

Sarah: I wasn't going to steal it.

Ralph: *(Crosses to bench, sits)* Man can't be too careful. *(The blueprint)* This is an important invention. I'm an important inventor.

Ginny: *(Enters from shanty)* It's a good thing I came back when I was needed. I put the clams in the refrigerator. *(Steps to Sarah)* I hope my brother hasn't been bothering you.

Ralph: I'm not your brother!

Ginny: You come down to visit your grandfather, hunh? *(Sarah nods)* Never knew a person who liked whales as much as him. Except maybe me. Whales need friends. Mr. Todd says he might take my brother and me to the movies one day next month. After his check comes in.

Sarah: He may not be here next month. *(Ginny and Ralph react. This is a possibility they hadn't considered. They don't like it)* He may be going home. That's why I'm here today. With my mother.

Ginny: You really mean Mr. Todd will be leaving?

Sarah: Could be.

Ginny: Oh, my goodness. *(Furious, Ralph jumps up and tears the blueprint in two)*

Ralph: Happens every time! Every time! You no sooner meet someone you can talk with, someone you think you can trust, and they run out on you!

Ginny: *(Matter-of-fact)* Ralph gets into these rages all the time.

Ralph: Shut up!

Ginny: That's why he has to see the therapist once a week.

Sarah: Therapist? Is he crazy or something? *(Dejected, Ralph sits on the bench, his face in his hands, groans)*

Ginny: *(Professionally)* He's "withdrawing."

Sarah: What?

Ginny: That's what the therapist told Mrs. Baker. Whenever my brother feels he doesn't have anyone to like him he crawls into his shell like a snail. Won't talk to anybody, won't do anything but sulk, sulk, sulk.

Sarah: I better tell my grandfather.

Ginny: Oh, he's used to Ralph. He says Ralph will come out of his shell when he's good and ready.

(Mrs. Baker enters Down Left. She is a pleasant woman, no nonsense type, a bit of a character. Wears a battered hat)

Ginny: Hi, Mrs. Baker.

Mrs. Baker: Hello, Ginny. Mr. Todd inside?

Sarah: I'll get him. *(Sarah enters cottage)*

Mrs. Baker: Who was that?

Ginny: Mr. Todd's granddaughter.

Mrs. Baker: She got a name?

Ginny: Sarah.

Mrs. Baker: Lovely old-fashioned name. Had an aunt named Sarah. *(She steps onto the porch)*

Ginny: Ralph's doing it again.

Mrs. Baker: *(Steps to him)* Ralph, what's the problem now? *(No response)* Remember what you're supposed to do when you feel like this – think of something positive.

Ginny: Won't do no good. *(Proud that she knows the psychological terminology)* He's withdrawn. He tore up his blueprint, too.

Grandpa: *(Enters, followed by Sarah)* Hello there, Mrs. Baker.

Mrs. Baker: *(She plucks a pair of eyeglasses from a pocket)* Figured you'd be needing these.

Grandpa: Bless you. I was tearing through the house looking for them.

Mrs. Baker: Left them at my place this morning when you stopped by for coffee. So, this is your granddaughter.

Grandpa: Sarah, this is Mrs. Baker.

Sarah: Hi.

Mrs. Baker: Hi.

Grandpa: What's the matter, Ralph?

Sarah: He's withdrawn.

Ginny: He heard you were going away, Mr. Todd.

Mrs. Baker: What? Who's going away? *(She sits in chair, Left, fans herself with her hat)* Getting hot.

Grandpa: Not for an ole Lalapalooza Bird.

Ginny: What kind of bird?

Grandpa: Lalapalooza. *(Suddenly, Ralph sits up straight)*

Ralph: There's no such bird! You made it up!

Mrs. Baker: Well, well, look who's back. Nice to have you with us, Ralph.

Ralph: I know all about birds! I'm an expert when it comes to birds. I could make a million dollars if I told everything I know about birds!

Mrs. Baker: If Mr. Todd says there's such a bird as a Lalapalooza, then it must be so.

Ginny: What kind of feathers does it have?

Sarah: What kind of a call does it make?

Grandpa: Everybody sit down and I'll show you. *(Eager, Sarah sits on the bench beside Ralph. Ginny plops onto the rocker. Grandpa steps Down Right. All eyes are on him)* The first thing you have to understand about the Lalapalooza Bird is that he likes to be free. He likes to stay active. He likes to make new friends. He likes to discover something different every day. He doesn't like to be caged in.

Sarah: I think that's called "imagination," Grandpa.

Ralph: He's not making it up. There is such a bird.

Ginny: Changed your mind in a hurry.

Mrs. Baker: If we keep expecting to see a whale, thanks to Mr. Todd, I don't see why we can't expect meet up with a Lalapalooza Bird.

Grandpa: The Lalapalooza's got some other unusual characteristics.

Ginny: Like what?

Grandpa: He likes to sing.

Sarah: What else?

Grandpa: The Lalapalooza is not a young bird. Except in spirit.

Mrs. Baker: *(Grins)* Go on.

Grandpa: It wants to keep on enjoying sunsets and sunrises. It wants to pass on some of the things it's learned about life. The good and the bad. That's what keeps it alive. *(By now it's pretty obvious to all that the Lalapalooza Bird and Grandpa are one and the same)*

Sarah: What does it sound like? *(All lean forward wondering how Grandpa will get out of this one)*

Grandpa: *(Rubs his chin)* Something like this. *(Pause. He cups his hand to his mouth and makes a "bird-like" call that sounds suspiciously like a barnyard citizen)*

Mrs. Baker: Must be kin to a rooster.

Grandpa: Best of all is its walk.

Ralph: Let's see it.

Grandpa: Comin' up! *(He prepares, working his arms and elbows like wings and stepping across the stage with the exaggerated gait of a large chicken. As he moves, he repeats the cry of the Lalapalooza. It's a comical moment and the onlookers are enjoying it immensely)*

Ad Libs: More, more! Looks like a chicken! Sounds like a rooster! Maybe it's looking for a worm!

Ralph: I could do that!

(Grandpa makes it to the bench, starts back across the stage. Ralph follows, imitating the Lalapalooza. Sarah follows Ralph. Ginny crosses behind the table and trails Sarah. Grandpa looks like a parent duck trailed by a family of ducklings. Mrs. Baker laughs. The "birds" continue to flap arms like wings, cry out, walk "funny," birdlike. Estelle appears Down Right. Grandpa sees her, stops, The other "birds" pile up!)

Ginny: Oops!

Grandpa: Oh, Estelle, Enjoy your walk?

Estelle: What on earth – ?

Ginny: Mr. Todd was showing us about the Lalapalooza Bird.

Estelle: The what?

Ralph: The Lalapalooza Bird. It's gotta be free. I know all about birds.

Ginny: *(Sees something on the beach, points)* Look! I think it's a sea lion washed up on the sand. *(All look)*

Mrs. Baker: *(Shades her eyes with her hat)* I don't see anything. Where?

Ginny: Down by the water's edge. It could be stranded or something. *(With great feeling)* It needs me! *(She runs out, Down Left)*

Ralph: Better get the lifeguard! *(He runs out after Ginny)*

Sarah: Wait for me! I'm coming, too! *(Sarah runs out)*

Estelle: Sarah!

Mrs. Baker: Ginny is a dear girl, but someday I hope she'll understand she can't be responsible for the world.

Grandpa: Estelle, honey, this is Mrs. Baker. Sit down, honey. *(He steps behind the rocker and holds it for Estelle. She sits)*

Estelle: My father says you take children in.

Mrs. Baker: You make it sound as if they were laundry.

Estelle: I didn't mean to.

Grandpa: Mrs. Baker has a license.

Estelle: License?

Mrs. Baker: I had to be approved by the state.

Estelle: I don't think I could handle children I didn't even know.

Mrs. Baker: That's what most people think. It's not true. Take Ginny and Ralph. Sometimes I think Ginny would drain all the love in the world if she could and I think Ralph would give up ten years of his life if he thought someone could love him and wanted him around.

Estelle: What about your own life?

Mrs. Baker: This is my life. My husband's gone. For a long time I wondered what I would do. Well, all the scientists tell us we're living longer and longer and I thought to myself I'd be a fool to let my life fritter away. So I decided to work with children. If I have love to give, I get plenty back. Your father coming here has been a blessing. Boy like Ralph needs special attention.

Estelle: My father couldn't possibly remain in this cottage during the winter.

Mrs. Baker: He can stay at my place. It's the biggest house on the beach.

Estelle: *(Weakly)* He has a lovely room at our apartment. Color television. *(Mrs. Baker and Grandpa exchange a concerned glance. Ralph stomps in Down Left)*

Ralph: That wasn't a sea lion!

Grandpa: What was it?

Ralph: A great big ole black inner tube.

Mrs. Baker: Well, maybe that great big ole black inner tube needs Ginny.

Grandpa: Got something for you, Ralph.

Ralph: What?

Grandpa: Remember what I told you about patience.

Ralph: I forgot.

Grandpa: To get patience you have to have patience. *(Grandpa exits into shanty.)*

Estelle: That's what he used to tell me when I was a little girl.

Ralph: It ain't true, is it?

Mrs. Baker: "Ain't" may be all right if you're planning on being a street bum, but if you're going to be as famous as you plan, you'd better speak good English.

Ralph: I meant to say – *(To Estelle)* It's not true, is it? Mr. Todd's not leaving us?

Estelle: *(Hesitates)* I don't know. *(Sarah and Ginny enter Down Left)*

Ginny: False alarm.

Sarah: It looked like a sea lion until you got up close.

Ralph: Didn't look like anything but what it was. A dirty ole inner tube. *(Grandpa comes from the shanty with a garment box)*

Grandpa: I hope you're going to like this, young fellow.

Ginny: I helped Grandpa pick it out. *(Grandpa puts the box on the table. Ralph steps in, curious)*

Mrs. Baker: Go on, Ralph. Open it.

Ralph: *(Guardedly)* What's in it?

Grandpa: One way to find out.

Ralph: You open it, Mr. Todd.

Grandpa: You have to open your own packages, Ralph.

Ginny: I'll open it.

Ralph: No!

Ginny: I wasn't going to steal it. If you ask me I don't think you even know what a gift is.

Ralph: Do so! One Christmas I got so many presents I couldn't even unwrap them all. *(Ralph remains apprehensive about the package. He summons up his courage and takes off the top. He moves aside the tissue paper, lifts out a handsome surfer's jacket, or beach windbreaker)*

Ginny: Now you can get out of that dirty old leather jacket.

Sarah: That's a surfer's jacket.

Mrs. Baker: It's a fine windbreaker, too.

Estelle: Put it on, Ralph. See if it fits.

Ralph: No! (*Impulsively, he puts the jacket back into the box and puts back the top*) I couldn't take off my leather. What would my friends think?

Ginny: What friends?

Ralph: You shut up, Ginny. I got more friends than anybody in the whole world!

Estelle: The least you might do is thank my father. (*Grandpa gestures to Estelle that this isn't necessary. Ralph takes the box, crosses to the bench, sits, sulks. To Grandpa*) Seems everyone knows why I'm here, so I don't see any point in delaying. I want you to come home, Dad. For good.

Ginny: Oh, no, Mr. Todd!

Estelle: I think what Mrs. Baker is doing is wonderful and generous. But it's only a passing fancy with you.

Grandpa: That's rubbish, Estelle. (*Mrs. Baker stands. The dialogue begins to sound like an argument*)

Mrs. Baker: Your father's happy here.

Estelle: Allow me to be the judge.

Grandpa: Estelle, don't talk like that. I'm not a child.

Ginny: (*Steps close to table*) You can't go away, Mr. Todd.

Estelle: Why can't he?

Ginny: Because he needs me.

Estelle: Sarah, you want your grandfather back, don't you?

Sarah: (*Steps by Ginny*) Yes, but –

Estelle: Yes, but, but, but – but what?

Sarah: He's happy here.

Estelle: I wish people would stop saying that.

Grandpa: I wish you could start saying it.

Mrs. Baker: Your father is doing a great deal of good.

Estelle: Talk sense, Mrs. Baker. What has he accomplished all the time he's been down here?

Sarah: Mother, that's unfair.

Estelle: It may be unfair, but it's the truth!

During the preceding argument, Ralph has taken the jacket from the box and removed his leather. He puts on the gift. No one notices. He steps Down Left. Grandpa is the first to notice, then Mrs. Baker, then Ginny and Sarah. They're amazed. Finally, even Estelle. Pause.

Ralph: *(Rubs his hand over jacket)* I, uh, thought I'd try it on. *(Pause)* For size. I may not like it.

Grandpa: Looks mighty handsome, Ralph.

Sarah: Now you look human. Sort of.

Estelle: *(Reluctant)* Seems I'm outnumbered. *(To Grandpa)* I'm not going to pretend I'm happy about this. I'm not, I'm not going to give up, either.

Mrs. Baker: *(The peacemaker)* You come along with me, Estelle, I want to show you my house. It's comfy. I'll put on the tea.

Estelle: We should be heading back.

Mrs. Baker: Plenty of time before dark. *(Holds out her hand)* Come along, dear. *(Estelle stiffens, nods. Mrs. Baker starts out, Down Left. Estelle follows)* The second story is never used and I've got six rooms up there. All furnished and empty. *(Mrs. Baker exits. Estelle stops, turns to her father. He smiles lovingly. Estelle exits. Sarah runs to her grandfather, embraces him)*

Sarah: I can visit you whenever I want!

Grandpa: You bet you can!

Ralph: *(Admires his new jacket)* It's not easy to cage a Lalapalooza Bird!

Grandpa: You're a bright lad, Ralph.

Ginny: But he needs me.

Grandpa: Hey, what do you think? Any whales out there yet?

Sarah: Let's look. *(Grandpa makes a "telescope" with his fists. Sarah, Ralph, and Ginny do the same. They group in front of table)*

Grandpa: Scan the horizon.

Ralph: What's that?

Ginny: You can be stupid, Ralph. It's where the sky and the earth appear to meet.

Ralph Who told you?

Ginny: Mr. Todd.

Grandpa: *(Steps behind the trio)* Any sign of a whale?

Sarah: Nope.

Ralph: Not yet.

Sarah: I wonder if we'll ever see one?

Grandpa: Use your imagination. Maybe we didn't see a whale yesterday –

Ginny and Ralph: *(Reciting)* – and maybe we won't see a whale today but that doesn't mean we won't see one tomorrow.

(Sarah makes the "cry" of the Lalapalooza Bird, followed by Ralph and Ginny. Grandpa hugs them close. They continue to "scan the horizon." Must be a whale out there somewhere.)

CURTAIN

Today A Little Extra

by Michael Kassin

Today A Little Extra

by Michael Kassin

Cast List
Mr. Abrams   Mrs. Finkelstein
Mr. Levine

Today A Little Extra

by Michael Kassin

The scene: A butcher shop, old, simple and on the verge of extinction. A picture window with words reads, "Zalman Abrams – Butcher"; the Hebrew word for kosher underneath. The window is gated as the story begins. Somewhere opposite this wall is a simple white butcher's display case and a counter with a scale on top. Behind the counter is a phone, and next to the phone, a sign – "Ask About Credit." Somewhere on this wall is the door to the back room in which the cooler, the chicken cages and who knows what else reside. Somewhere onstage are three old chrome chairs with green vinyl seats – in a row – meant to seat impatient customers who, alas, no longer come.

It is 8 a.m. Through this doorway comes Zalman Abrams, 74, whitehaired, stooped but apparently healthy. He takes a long look at the counter top; he taps the scale with his fingers; he unlocks the gated window and door. He disappears for a moment into the back room. He reappears, coat off, skullcap on, bloody apron in hand, pencil behind the ear. He shuts his eyes and says a quick prayer. He opens them again and dons the apron. Again he disappears for a moment. The sound of an old radio is heard, more static than sound – the kind you heard in barber shops when you were a kid. He re-enters carrying a broom and a piece of cardboard. He sweeps, hums, smiles, looks at the piece of cardboard. It is a sign, "Under New Management." He drops it onto the floor and sweeps everything onto it. He disappears again to dispose of the dirt. The phone rings. With much grumbling, he picks it up.

Abrams: Boo-tcher! . . . Who? . . . Candy's Massage Parlor? No, I'm sorry, this is kosher meat. *(He hangs up and starts for the back room. The phone rings again. He picks it up.)* . . . Hallo? You again? Look, I don't know from Candy, but if you can reach her at 8 a.m., she's in the wrong business . . . *(starts to hang up again)* . . . Who? Max Levine? It didn't sound like you . . . It didn't sound like me either? What do you know, a stranger could make a good living talking to you . . . So, how's the delicatessen? . . . From you either they don't buy kosher meat? . . . Well, at least you got trafe meat you can sell to make a living . . . Must be good for the pocketbook to be a liberal . . . So? How should I feel on the last day? Ya, big plans . . . Monday I'm running away with an 18-year-old girl . . . yeah, a real tzatzke . . . Why? We're good for one another. With what I got, and what she's got, we'll get along like Richard Burton and Elizabeth Schwartzkopf . . . So what can I do for you? . . . Ya, I'll be out today . . .

103

Who are you sending over? The boy? If he's like you, I wouldn't let him in . . . He's taking the shop? We'll see. A little test I'll give him . . . *(Mark Levine appears at the door.)* You're wrong, he's not on his way, because I think that's him at the door now . . . How do I know? Same guilty look as you had before you got rich . . . I'll talk to you . . . Goodbye . . .

He hangs up. Mark Levine enters. He is about 27, fairly well-dressed — except that his suit is a little too tight on his chubby body. He is a good boy, but he's trying too hard to come across as a worldly 40-year-old executive. He carries his topcoat in his hand. Abrams has him sized up in three seconds.

Levine: Mr. Abrams –

Abrams: *(cutting him off)* Yes? Don't tell me. You wife sent you early you shouldn't wake the guests –

Levine: Mr. Abrams –

Abrams: – and the A & P ain't open yet, and besides, they ain't got kosher like Zalman Abrams got kosher so you come by me to get the best. You're new in the neighborhood?

Levine: No, I –

Abrams: I know, don't say it. You had a fight. You had a fight, you didn't want to spend extra, and your wife sent you anyway . . . We dicker, ya? Like in the old days. I cheat you, and you starve me. You're my first customer, no one would know the difference. What do you want? Chicken? I got one in this morning, so big I had to circumsize the door to bring it in –

Levine: *(smiling but addled)* No, thank you –

Abrams: You'd like maybe beef? I got brisket, so tender, so delicious – let me tell you. Kissinger bought by me kosher brisket and served it to the Arabs – half of them converted . . .

Levine: Mr. Abrams –

Abrams: Duck . . . You start now, maybe it would be ready for Shabbos. So much pleasure you'll get from eating this bird, you wouldn't look at your wife for a week.

Levine: Please –

Abrams: You don't like so fancy? I give you steak . . . Good, simple steak, like the goyem eat when they go by Sardi's. No class, but very tasty.

Levine: Just let me –

Abrams: – think about it? Of course you think about it. You go call your wife. Go, go, go . . . There's a phone on the corner. You think it over. She'll know what is best. You have guests, a happy meal this should be . . . *(Levine is about to give up.)* . . . You want everything? I could make by you a special price. This is my last day you know.

Levine: *(spotting his chance)* I know.

Abrams: You know?

Levine: *(extending his hand)* I'm Mark Levine.

Abrams: *(unbelievingly taking it)* You're Levine?

Levine: Mark. *(He smiles.)*

Abrams: But Max Levine –

Levine: – is my father.

Abrams: Max said he would send by me the new manager.

Levine: And owner. *(He glows.)*

Abrams: And Manny?

Levine: Manny will stay at Pa's shop and help when I need him.

Abrams: Manny don't get the shop?

Levine: Manny didn't want the shop. Manny has a bad heart.

Abrams: And you got the shop, huh? . . . *(He looks at Levine.)* How old are you?

Levine: Older than you when you started.

Abrams: How do you know?

Levine: Pa told me.

Abrams: Your pa counts like he weighs meat. No wonder he's got such a big business . . . He and I started the same age.

Levine: That's not what he said.

Abrams: Who you gonna believe – your father or an honest man?

Levine: Can we get down to business?

Abrams: Ya, what can I do for you?

Levine: Can we talk seriously?

Abrams: Wait a minute . . . *(He exits to the back room for a moment. The radio is turned to solid static and the volume is turned up. He reappears.)* . . . Ya?

Levine: Uh, can we turn that off so we can start?

Abrams: I thought you wanted to talk serious?

Levine: I do.

Abrams: So, why are you making me play games with the radio?

Levine: *(exasperated)* . . . Please –

Abrams: You want me to turn it off?

Levine: Thank you, yes.

Abrams: Okay, I be right back . . . *(He disappears. A long pause as Mark tries to busy himself. Then loud crashes from offstage. Finally silence.)*

Levine: *(calling after him)* Mr. Abrams . . . Mr. Abrams! . . . Mr. Abrams!

Abrams: *(offstage)* Not yet; my tuchas ain't got ears. *(The radio is turned off. He re-enters.)* Now, Mr. Levine.

Levine: Mr. Abrams, I've thought –

Abrams: So have I. You come tomorrow, ya? The shop is yours tomorrow. It's in the papers.

Levine: Please. I've planned this very carefully –

Abrams: So have I. Thirty-four years I've been in this shop, and on my last day here I close at 5:30. You come tomorrow, ya? This shop is yours tomorrow. It's all in the papers.

Levine: The thing is, if I can get an early start, I could maybe be open Monday.

Abrams: Monday you want to be open?

Levine: Yes.

Abrams: So work on Sunday.

Levine: Who works on Sunday?

Abrams: Kind men who don't kick Alta Kakers out before the time has come. Listen to me. Today you go and think some more. Tomorrow you pray the shop should keep you like it's kept me. Sunday you do a little extra, ya?

Levine: Thirty-one years Pa's run his shop, even a delicatessen, he's never worked on Sunday.

Abrams: So?

Levine: So now I have a shop. Sunday I don't work.

Abrams: Ya, and a year from Sunday you go broke. You want to be ready Monday? Sunday you do a little extra.

Levine: Today I'll do extra. Tomorrow I'll do extra. Sunday I don't work.

Abrams: But Saturday you work?

Levine: *(nodding)* Saturday I work. Saturday is the biggest day of the week.

Abrams: I know. Saturday I don't work.

Levine: Yeah, and look at you – *(He stops himself. Abrams moves to the window, and with great patience, motions to Levine.)*

Abrams: Come here, sonny boy. Come. Look across the street. See? With the windows boarded, with the words I'm trying not to read? Thirty-four years ago it was Mandelman's Grocery Store. Mandelman dies and young Mandelman takes over. Six years. Then it's Warshawski's Sausages and Fine Meats. Nineteen years maybe. Warshawski retires. Now it's Young's Rib Tips with Extra Hot Sauce. Three years. Young is robbed twice in a month. He sells to Lopez. I don't know what Lopez sells; I can't read the sign. Lopez is evicted by the city, who makes it an office for a nice boy with too much hair and not enough sense. The office is burned. Now it sits empty. Thirty-four years I'm here and I don't work Shabbos. Listen to me. Sunday you do a little extra. Today you leave me alone, ya?

Levine: Look, Mr. Abrams, in half an hour they're making a delivery from my father's shop. I thought if I could get –

Abrams: They're making a delivery? Today? In my shop?

Levine: Yes.

Abrams: What kind of delivery?

Levine: What do you think?

Abrams: I don't know. From your father's shop it could be maybe pigeon parts in chili sauce.

Levine: My father sells good meat.

Abrams: With his customer, who would know the difference?

Levine: Look, I'm not going to argue with you. I just want to know –

Abrams: Is it kosher?

Levine: What?

Abrams: This meat they're delivering. Is it kosher?

Levine: Who's going to buy kosher meat in this neighborhood anymore?

Abrams: *(shrugging)* I don't know. Must be a rich phantom kept me in business so long.

Levine: Please, this is the only time I can get him to deliver.

Abrams: You have him deliver tomorrow, ya? I'll be in the Synagogue. I wouldn't look.

Levine: He's not working tomorrow.

Abrams: I'm glad to see somebody there had got some sense.

Levine: Look, I won't be in your way. You can sell what you want. In twenty-four hours it'll be my shop anyway, so what difference does it make?

Abrams: What difference does it make? In five minutes will come Esther Finkelstein to buy for Shabbos, who has been my customer since before her husband died. Twenty-six years years she's come to me because I run a kosher shop. Three blocks away is the A&P which is selling kosher meat for cheap maybe ten years now, from which she don't buy because also they sell trafe. Tomorrow there will be no place and she will be your problem. Today there is still a place, and after twenty-six years, she is still my problem – and I want it that way.

Levine: Mr. Abrams –

Abrams: No.

Levine: Just listen a minute.

Abrams: The answer is no.

Levine: She'll be gone before he gets here with the delivery, so what's the problem?

Abrams: She'll be back. You don't know the ritual.

Levine: The ritual?

Abrams: Stick around.

Levine: What does she care what's being delivered?

Abrams: I care, and I ain't gonna disappoint her.

Levine: Look, can I use your phone?

Abrams: Are you gonna cancel the delivery?

Levine: No.

Abrams: Then use the one on the street. Cost you twenty-five cents. Unless maybe the kids fixed it again. Then it don't cost you nothing.

Levine: They do things like that in this neighborhood?

Abrams: What do you mean, "in this neighborhood?" In Queens they don't cheat the phone company?

Levine: If you'll excuse me.

Abrams: It's all right.

Levine: I'll be back, very soon.

Abrams: Take your time. I got all day.

Levine: We'll see.

Abrams: What? You'll get your father after me? What can he do? By the time he gets his lawyer I could elope with Mrs. Finkelstein. And what's the point of that? We're both sterile. Relax boychik. Monday you'll be open anyway and this will all be funny when you think about it.

Levine: You think so?

Abrams: Ya. With a pest like you around, your papa will either get by you the meat or cancel your birth certificate. Go make your call.

Levine: I'll be back. *(He exits. Abrams watches him for a moment, then goes to the phone and dials Max Levine's number.)*

Abrams: Hallo? Max? . . . Look your boy just left me . . . Ya, he said he'd be right back . . . I don't know; he's probably trying to call you now . . . Why? If he don't learn to open his mouth, he'll be out of business in a week . . . Ya, he's a nice boy, but he don't know how to talk . . . How hard on him could I be? If he thinks I'm bad, wait 'til he hears the Wailing Widow . . . *(and who should appear at the door)* Oy, mention the devil and she taps you on the shoulder. I'll talk to you. Goodbye. *(He hangs up, bangs the phone. The coins return.)* Esther Finkelstein enters. She is a small, not unattractive woman of 68. She is dressed simply in a black overcoat, blue dress and blue pillbox hat.) Today of all days, you had to be first?

Finkelstein: *(looking around)* Wait. I'll stand back from the door I shouldn't get trampled. *(She takes a deep breath)* Oy, such a crowd is here I could die of suffocation.

Abrams: Very funny.

Finkelstein: Funny? I'm funny? With what you sell me, I don't know whether to cook it or have it arrested. What have you got for me fresh?

Abrams: Take a number and find out.

Finkelstein: What's to take a number for? There's no one here.

Abrams: After twenty six years, you want to spoil the system?

Finkelstein: No, I can see how well it's working. *(She takes a number)* Here. Five. You happy now? *(Abrams looks at his "number machine.")*

Abrams: *(loudly)* Two! Where is two, please?

Finkelstein: You mean I gotta wait? I'll be back in half an hour.

Abrams: Don't be so long, you'll lose your place in line.

Finkelstein: I'm going by the A&P.

Abrams: Why?

Finkelstein: What do you mean, why? I need eggs.

Abrams: I got eggs fresh.

Finkelstein: Huh. You "fresh eggs" are already on pension.

Abrams: I'll give you fresh as I got. Why are you going by the A&P?

Finkelstein: Why? Next week will be a new owner here and I'll have to go anyway. I thought today I would practice.

Abrams: You can't practice later?

Finkelstein: I can practice now while I'm waiting for you.

Abrams: I'll bring out another tray. I'm sorry I ain't had time yet.

Finkelstein: You ain't had time yet? Why not?

Abrams: The new owner was in.

Finkelstein: *(excited)* Really? What does he look like?

Abrams: You're too old for him . . . You're finally giving up on me?

Finkelstein: What hope have I got? Twelve years I'm trying to get you to come for Sabbath dinner at my apartment, and every week it's a different excuse. So what is it this time?

Abrams: What is it this time? I'm too old for fast women. *(He exits.)*

Finkelstein: Tomorrow you'll be younger?

Abrams: Have a seat. I'll be right back.

Finkelstein: Take your time. The A & P ain't open yet . . . Huh. It would serve you right if I left and bought from them.

Abrams: *(offstage)* Have a seat and rest your mouth. *(She sits on a row of old green chairs across from the counter.)*

Finkelstein: Oy, the way you talk, anyone would think we were married.

Abrams: *(offstage)* Huh. The way you talk back, anyone would know better.

Finkelstein: In your house a wife can't speak her piece?

Abrams: *(returning with two trays of meat)* In my house, my wife always spoke her piece. So did I. That's why she's dead fourteen years and I'm still around. Here *(He motions to the trays.)* . . . You want fancy on the last day, or just the usual?

Finkelstein: I can't afford the usual. Why should I pay extra for the fancy? . . . Unless, of course, you're making me a special price.

Abrams: Special price? I'll give you a special price. You still owe me from before. On the last day you'll pay the balance?

Finkelstein: On the last day I'll maybe pay the balance if you'll give me extra.

Abrams: I'll give you "extra." If you don't pay up today, I'll come over and collect.

Finkelstein: *(sighing)* Twelve years I been waiting to hear you say that.

Abrams: Okay, okay, what do you want extra?

Finkelstein: Let me see maybe a nice piece of chuck.

Abrams: Chuck? *(He removes one from the tray, puts it on the counter,)* I got for you a chuck roast. Let me tell you —

Finkelstein: You told me. Twelve years you've been telling me. Keep it a little while yet. You can give it a nice Bar Mitzvah. Let me see . . . *(She handles it.)* Huh. The cow that gave you this is still laughing. Where is the meat? All I see is bone, and where the bone ain't, the gristle is.

Abrams: On your credit you were expecting eye of the rib?

Finkelstein: On my credit I was expecting something I could swallow. Let me see chicken. *(Abrams starts to remove one from a tray.)* Uh-uh. Let me see fresh!

Abrams: Wait a minute. *(He disappears for a moment. She goes to the scale and taps it.)*

Finkelstein: Once, just once on the last day, you'll give an honest weight? . . . Ah, what am I talking? You're like he is – too old to change. *(Abrams re-enters on this last, chicken in hand.)*

Abrams: What are you doing with my trusty scale?

Finkelstein: "Trusty scale", huh? If God weighed souls like that, the devil would be taking lessons. Let me see your scrawny hen . . . (*He gives it to her. She runs her hands over it, then, like a surgeon, begins to pinch and finger it very carefully.*)

Abrams: What are you going to do, eat it or molest it?

Finkelstein: (*holding it up to him*) You're selling it. Why should you care?

Abrams: You don't like? I got others.

Finkelstein: Let me see fresh.

Abrams: You mean live? You'll have to wait for the Shochet. He ain't here to slaughter 'em.

Finkelstein: When will he be?

Abrams: I don't know. Maybe ten o'clock. It used to be he was here all day Friday. Now he gives me maybe a couple of hours when he can spare them.

Finkelstein: And what about your customers?

Abrams: There ain't so many any more. And them what takes, takes like you take.

Finkelstein: How can you run a business like that?

Abrams: I can't. That's why I'm retiring . . . You want to look at another?

Finkelstein: Ya. Something with some meat on it. (*He removes one from a hook. She starts to object.*)

Abrams: It's all right. It's fresh from yesterday. Here. (*She looks at it, fingers it, pinches it like the other.*)

Finkelstein: This is better, but it ain't so clean.

Abrams: Huh, missus, you should pass such a physical.

Finkelstein: This is all you got?

Abrams: Tell you what. You take this one, I give you a dozen eggs free.

Finkelstein: Sold! . . . Wait . . . Let me see the eggs. (*He hands her a carton.*) Three of them is broken.

Abrams: What do you want from a bargain chicken? If they were unbroken, I'd sell them. You're gonna take it?

Finkelstein: All right. All right. Throw in the eggs and this one I'll take . . . Abrams, what is three unbroken eggs on the last day? (*Pause*)

Abrams: You're right. (*And he gives here three replacements.*) . . . Now you got a dozen good eggs free . . . (*He shows her.*) . . . and a chicken without a gizzard. (*He shows her that too.*)

Finkelstein: I give up. Cut for me the chicken please.

Abrams: All right. (*He starts to.*)

Finkelstein: Ah-ah You won't forget to weigh for me please?

Abrams: *sighing* All right. (*He puts the chicken on the scale. She puts her nose up to the scale and watches very carefully.*)

Finkelstein: Fingers away from the scale please . . . (*Grumbling, he does so. She looks at the scale, leaning over to check his side and then her own.*) . . . How come on my side is three pounds and yours is only two-and-a-half?

Abrams: Must be the way you're staring. I got here a sensitive machine. You stare too long, it skimps . . . (*They exchange looks.*)

Finkelstein: Cut for me the chicken please. (*He does so, the old way, with a large knife. He begins to wrap it.*) And don't forget any parts like last time.

Abrams: How could I? Three days afterwards the gizzard yelled at me in your voice. What kind of power you got over chickens? (*He has wrapped it now, and he is tying it with a string.*) Three-fifteen please.

Finkelstein: Three-fifteen? How much a pound is chicken?

Abrams: Same as last time.

Finkelstein: Then how come it don't cost like last time? Twenty-six years the chickens have been getting smaller, and the prices bigger, and always the cost is the "same as last time." Who are you kidding?

Abrams: I ain't kidding. It don't cost more. It's the taxes that cost more. If you don't like, take your chicken to City Hall and get back the difference.

Finkelstein: Huh, a lot of good that would do me. One look at us, they'd put me in a rest home and the chicken on relief. Ah, just once I wish I could afford a nice roast.

Abrams: Why not? With what you owe already, a little more ain't gonna break either of us.

Finkelstein: What's the sense of it? A chicken already lasts by me a week. How long do you think a roast would keep?

Abrams: Invite a guest . . . (*She looks at him.*) I mean one who would come.

Finkelstein: What's the use? Them what ain't dead are cowards like you.

Abrams: With what you cook, small wonder.

Finkelstein: You sell it. You should talk. (*Levine re-enters.*)

Abrams: Here's the eggs. This is maybe enough for one Friday, or you'll be back like usual?

Finkelstein: You want to spoil the ritual?

Abrams: No, I know too well – (*He stops.*) . . . Uh, Mrs. Finkelstein, this is Mark Levine, the new owner.

Finkelstein: Owner? I thought maybe a new delivery boy. What's a pisher like you doing in a business like this?

Levine: (*smiling*) Trying to make an honest living.

Finkelstein: Huh. That's what Abrams told me. And look at his business. And he cheats good. You don't look like you cheat so good.

Levine: I won't need to.

Finkelstein: Why not? Your daddy's name is Rockefeller? Boychik, believe, me, in a business like this, you do a little extra. What they don't know don't hurt them, and what they do know, they usually accept – right Abrams? *(No response.)* Well, I see you . . . *(She starts to go)* . . . So, Mr. Levine, you'll have kosher for me next week? If not, I got no place to go . . . *(Again she starts to leave.)* And healthy. Not like Abrams sells. You look at his hens, you don't know whether to eat them or adopt them . . . Well, I see you . . . *(She exits. Abrams and Levine stare after her.)*

Levine: You have many customers like her?

Abrams: No, thank God. She's all I can afford . . . Well?

Levine: Well what?

Abrams: You couldn't wait until tomorrow?

Levine: That's what I wanted to talk to you about. I spoke with my dad –

Abrams: So did I.

Levine: You did?

Abrams: Ya. Before you got here. And after. In fact, he told me you were coming.

Levine: So, why did you pretend –

Abrams: A little test I gave you. You failed. You're not ready to run a shop. Listen to me. Manny could come and help for a while –

Levine: Manny couldn't get away right now. Not for that long. A day or two maybe, but you're talking a month, two months. Dad couldn't spare him that long.

Abrams: That's what I figured. Well, I could help. It would ease the transition.

Levine: You? Why would you want to help? You're retiring. I thought you were sick of this.

Abrams: After five minutes of the Wailing Widow I'm too angry to be sick. Anyway, with two of us here it wouldn't be so bad. You could deliver –

Levine: I'm not going to deliver. The delivery boy will deliver. How am I going to learn the business if I'm out delivering?

Abrams: Okay, so you'll hire a delivery boy. Simpler yet. Three people to do the work of one. Think what a business we can build.

Levine: We?

Abrams: You and me. I can teach you shortweight, who to cheat and who not, how to cut skimpy –

Levine: What I need I can learn from Dad. And what's this "we" business? The shop is mine, isn't it?

Abrams: *(sadly)* Ya, the shop is yours.

Levine: So sooner or later, I'm going to have to learn from my own mistakes, right?

Abrams: Right.

Levine: So it might as well be sooner. Like today, right? *(No answer.)* Now, I talked to my father. The way we figured it, between your delivery boy and our delivery boy, we could –

Abrams: What delivery boy?

Levine: You mean you don't have a delivery boy?

Abrams: Ya, I have a delivery boy. I've had eight delivery boys in two years. Now I have no delivery boy. Six months maybe. Why do you think I'm selling.

Levine: Why didn't you say something? Dad could have worked something out.

Abrams: Why should he waste his time? Anyway, what difference does it make? If I had said something, you wouldn't have a shop.

Levine: I'd have waited a year or two.

Abrams: A year or two? *(Laughing)* Boychik, if I'd had help here I could trust, they would bury me in this shop. You think I'd give up that easy?

Levine: No, I guess not . . . What makes you so stubborn?

Abrams: What makes me so stubborn? You think through Mandelman and Warshawsky and Young and Lopez that Abrams would have stayed if he hadn't been stubborn? You think I'd last two minutes with Mrs. Finkelstein if I wasn't stubborn? *(He winks at Levine.)* Stick with me. I'll make you so stubborn your worst enemy would buy from you extra. And like it.

Levine: Mr. Abrams, I've – *(Pause)* Look. All right. So our delivery boy will deliver. If you haven't delivered in six months, there can't be so many –

Abrams: Please . . .

Levine: Do you have a list?

Abrams: Ya, I got a list . . . *(He goes behind the counter and produces a small, battered pocket book.)*

Levine: Let me see –

Abrams: Ah! Ah! *(He jerks it away.)* It ain't up to date yet . . . *(He thumbs through.)* . . . Abramowitz . . . Huh. She passed away six months ago . . . Aronberg . . . They moved to Florida . . . On what I don't know. They still owe me $26.37 . . . Levy, ah, they come on and off –

Levine: Mr. Abrams, do you know how many you've got?

114

Abrams: *(shrugging)* What's the sense of counting 'til they've bought? If·they come, I got chickens enough. If not, let it rest. It's between them and their souls . . . *(Pause)* What do you got, Boychik? Do you got kosher? *(He taps his heart.)* . . . In here I mean . . . *(No answer.)* So how can you deliver to them what has? How can you run a shop for them? How can you take "Zalman Abrams – Kosher Butcher" and make it "Mark Levine – Trafe"?

Levine: *(a little perturbed)* Mr. Abrams, I'm taking over a business. You make it sound like I'm turning a Synagogue into Burger King.

Abrams: *(a wry smile)* Not bad, not bad. You're not so dumb as I thought . . .

Levine: Look, Mr. Abrams, what's so terrible about trying to make a buck?

Abrams: In this neighborhood it's like birth control. Look boychik. Your father bought for you a shop in a lousy neighborhood. Why? You think he wants you to turn it into another B. Manischevitz and Company?

Levine: Is it such a sin to try?

Abrams: He wants you to learn a business, right? So that someday you can run his place, right? Now why would he pick a dying shop in a lousy neighborhood, huh? *(He is interrupted by the reappearance of Mrs. Finkelstein.)* . . . Now you had to come, ya? I'm trying to make sense to this pisher, who don't want to keep a kosher shop. What do you want, another chicken or more eggs?

Finkelstein: Neither. Give me the stringy chuck roast, please.

Abrams: *(incredulous)* Instead of the chicken?

Finkelstein: Who said a word about the chicken? The chicken is mine . . . *(Looking at Levine.)* If the pisher ain't gonna sell kosher, I got to stock up.

Abrams: You're only planning on living another week?

Finkelstein: In another week I'll find another place. At least this way I got time to think. Give me what you want. On the last day, I ain't even going to argue . . . *(Abrams begins to work, and she speaks to Levine.)* . . . Boychik, let me tell you about Abrams . . . *(She shrugs.)* So all right. So he shortweights a little. So once in a while we shortchange him in return. It balances out . . . *(Abrams looks at her.)* . . . *(To Levine)* . . . Look at this neighborhood . . . Believe me, the pocketbooks look like the buildings . . . Them what has, leave when they can. Them what hasn't stays . . . So who would want to run a business in this? . . . You never get ahead . . . Always they owe you . . . With what they owe Abrams, he should have a house in Florida by now. *(smiling)* . . . Huh. With what he charges, he should own the state . . . You know what? "So they owe me," he says. "Let it rest. They have a good Sabbath and I have a good business. Over pennies you don't break a friendship." . . . *(Pause)* So, for all of us, today I buy from him extra . . . *(By now, Abrams has weighed the meat and is wrapping it.)*

Abrams: Four thirty-six please . . .

Finkelstein: Here. *(She gives him a ten dollar bill.)* Keep the change.

Abrams: Esther –

Finkelstein: What? I know what I'm doing.

Abrams: I know better. This is grocery money for the week. I can't take this.

Finkelstein: Take.

Abrams: I can't.

Finkelstein: Take! *(Her voice is very fierce.)* . . . So for one week I'll skimp on milk and spend on meat. For me there will be other weeks. This much I can do . . . *(She looks at him and smiles.)* . . . Five dollars extra. Is that so much? . . . Twenty-four years ago you took my son off the street and made an apprentice out of him. You took a boy out of jail and gave me back a Mensch . . . *(to Levine)* . . . My son died in Korea. At the end . . . I got from him a medal for his death. I gave the medal to Abrams . . . You still have it?

Abrams: I still have it.

Finkelstein: *(to Levine)* You see? . . . For a few ounces extra, I forgive . . . You understand? *(Pause)* . . . Abrams, you thief you, for five dollars extra you'll maybe come tonight for Shabbos dinner? I'll be waiting. I'm going home now to start . . . *(She starts for the door. As she gets to it, she turns to Abrams once more. There is a quaver in her voice.)* . . . Old man, I love you . . . *(And she exits.)* *(A long pause. Abrams, tears in his eyes, begins to sweep again for want of something to do. Levine stands for a long moment looking at Abrams. Then he moves to the phone and dials.)*

Levine: Hello? Dad? This is Mark . . . Fine, fine . . . Listen. Have Ziggy hold up on the delivery . . . What? No, no problems; I'll explain it later. Ya, fine fine. Ya, sure, everything's okay. No, no time now . . . I'll see you. Goodbye . . . *(Abrams has turned to look at him.)* Mr. Abrams, I want you to come in next week. I want you to come as often as you like. Please . . . I think I understand now . . .

Abrams: *(smiling)* You'll be out of business in a month.

Levine: I'll make it . . .

Abrams: I did . . . *(Pause)* . . . Huh. Business. I couldn't cheat an Arab now if he paid me double . . . *(And he looks outside.)*

Levine: *(looking at Abrams and smiling)* I could . . . want to teach me? *(Abrams looks back at Levine and smiles.)*

Abrams: You? You don't even know what kosher is.

Levine: *(smiling)* I do. Really. *(He taps his heart and smiles.)* *(Now it is Abrams' turn to smile. He moves toward Levine, then past Levine to the phone. He bangs on the phone. The coins return. He hands them to Levine.)*
Lights fade out.

Emissary

by Doris M. Vineberg

Emissary

by Doris M. Vineberg

Cast List

Sam	Francesca	Anne
Lloyd	Scott	Rosie
Roxanne	Sophie	

Emissary

by Doris M. Vineberg

An elderly Jewish gentleman is sitting along on a park bench. A well dressed young man, about 30, approaches the bench.

Lloyd: Excuse me, are you expecting someone?

Sam: Sit down, young man.

Lloyd: *(muttering)* Young . . . young.

Sam: What else? Sure young. You have your whole life ahead of you.

Lloyd: *(angrily)* 20 benches in this goddam Garden of Eden and I have to sit next to St. Francis of Assisi!! What do you know about it?

Sam: I maybe said something wrong?

Lloyd: Forget it . . . how old are you?

Lloyd: How old am I? I'm maybe 79-81-82.

Lloyd: Don't you know?

Sam: Not exactly.

Lloyd: You mean you don't know when your birthday is?

Sam: Who knows from birthdays.

Lloyd: Strange. My wife, Anne, and I are so big on birthdays. We feel it's a very special day. It's the day that you were born.

Sam: My grandchildren have birthdays. Me? I don't know from them. What difference does it make anyhow. I'm old. You're young. You have your birthday, I have my deathday. –

Lloyd: Death?

Sam: Sure, death.

Lloyd: Why should I think about dying?

Sam: Dying is a part of living.

Lloyd: *(stands up angrily)* Listen, you have lived your whole life. You're old. 79-81-82 that's it! There's nothing else!! *(Realizes what he has said, sits down and buries his head in his hands. After several moments, he looks up.)* I'm . . . I'm sorry.

119

Sam: Don't be foolish. Six months ago I thought I was young. Today, I am an old man. *(Several moments of silence)* I like this bench. I always sit on this bench. You come here often? Never saw you before.

Lloyd: No, never before. Never had time.

Sam: You know, it's a funny thing. Six months ago, I never had time. I used to pass and see all old people sitting here doing nothing. You know, I found out something. Just because they look like they're doing nothing, doesn't mean that they're doing nothing. Know what I mean?

Lloyd: No.

Sam: There are all empty benchs around. Why did you sit here?

Lloyd: I don't know.

Sam: You know what I was doing?

Lloyd: No.

Sam: I was learning to be at peace with myself. This is not an easy thing to do. It takes a lot of "doing nothing" time. *(Silence)* Six months ago today I lost my Jennie.

Lloyd: I'm sorry.

Sam: Ah – what a woman.

Lloyd: What did she die from?

Sam: She starved to death.

Lloyd: In this day and age?

Sam: Blocked off passage. The food couldn't go through.

Lloyd: That's ridiculous. Nobody starves to death.

Sam: You're telling me no; I'm telling you yes. Cancer. They could have kept here alive for a few more months. Maybe she'd even be here today.

Lloyd: Then why didn't they?

Sam: She wouldn't let them. She said she didn't want to see me suffer.

Lloyd: She was the one dying, but she didn't want to see you suffer.

Same: Some woman.

Lloyd: How . . . how did she know? That she was dying, I mean?

Sam: One day, in the hospital, the doctor comes into her room. "Good Morning, Jennie," he says. "Dr. Fiore," she says, "sit down. I want to talk to you." You know how those doctors run in and out and you can't say a word to them. Anyhow, she says, "Tell me the truth. Because if I'm dying, I want to go home." "Now, Jennie," he says . . . and she says, "Don't 'now, Jennie' me. I have business to attend to. I . . . I want to die in my own bed with my Sam beside me." The next day she came home by ambulance. *(Several moments pass.)* You know what business she had to attend to? She had to make sure that Marilyn, that's our daughter, got

120

her silver and cut glass pieces, and Rachel, my son's wife got her diamond ring. It always bothered Jennie that my son never gave his wife a diamond. Jennie wanted to see the pleasure while she was alive.

Lloyd: Anne is like that, too. Always concerned about me. Actually, I always felt we had something special going for us.

Sam: Don't we all? If I could have those years back again . . . oy.

Lloyd: We have a boy, seven, and a girl, five, just the way we planned it.

Sam: A millionaire's family, they say. I was so busy making a living, who had time to even know the children?

Lloyd: Disneyland. I've got to get them to Disneyland. I promised them.

Sam: 51 years we were married. How do you like that? 51 years.

Lloyd: We were married 9 years in June. We . . . did . . . did she suffer much?

Sam: Thank God, no. She was hungry and weak, but thank God, no pain.

Lloyd: What about you? Did you talk about it?

Sam: What else? That's all Jennie wanted to do was talk. I kept saying, "Jennie, Jennie, you're going to get better." She'd take my hand and say, "Sam, don't be such a 'nahr'". That means fool . . . anyhow she said, "We've got to talk and it will be much easier for you when I'm gone." And she was right.

Lloyd: 9 years . . . what happened to those 9 years?

Sam: Funny thing, our marriage was arranged. That's the way they did things in those days. We got married, had children, lived together, but we nevertalked. We never said what was on our minds. In those last few days, while she was home, we got to know one another. I mean really got to know.

Lloyd: That all sounds so happy, you'd think you were talking about a birth, not a death. It's almost obscene!! My God, man, she was dying!!

Sam: I didn't know. I wanted to die myself. What was life without her? Listen, boychick, it doesn't make any difference if you are married 50 years or 5 years. If it was up to the young people they would say that everyone should die in order of their age. All neat and arranged. But it doesn't happen that way. I had Jennie for 51 years but what I'm trying to tell you is that only when she was dying did I come to realize what I had. You're lucky. You've got your wife, your children and time. Use it!

Lloyd: St. Francis, again.

Sam: Oy, boychick, you don't understand. I remember one day she was crying. Was she in pain, I asked. "No," she said, "not physical pain." She was quiet for a while. "Sam," she said, "I'm not going to see our first great grandchild." What could I say? Then she said, "But there's always unfinished business."

Lloyd: I guess so. I suppose when you think about yourself dying you have to be philosophical . . . protect yourself.

Sam: Death comes . . . living is difficult. You have to work at living. You just can't sit there and wait for life to come to you. She taught me that. Like I said, Jennie was some kind of a woman.

Lloyd: Somehow I almost feel as though I knew her.

Sam: When she was alive, everyone felt that way. They were standing in the synagogue at her funeral because all the seats were taken. People came I never even knew. Do you know, years ago, Jennie took out an insurance policy on the children. In those days, you paid 50¢ a week and the insurance man came to the house to collect. You know how many years ago that was? That insurance man came to the funeral. Can you imagine that?

Lloyd: Insurance . . .*(becomes very preoccupied)*

Sam: Well, young man, I must be going now. *(gets up)* If I'm not back, my daughter worries. I live with her now, so sometimes I behave like one of her children. *(Sam shoots Lloyd a long wink)* Maybe I'll see you here again sometimes? *(No response, so Sam slowly walks off stage breaking into a jig step, one time just before he disappears from view)*

Lloyd: Goodbye, old man. If what the doctor told me is true . . . no, my friend, I don't think so.

FINIS

SCENE TWO

Another afternoon. Sam is sitting on the park bench as a young girl, walks by and trips.

Francesca: Oh, damn . . .

Sam: *(picking her up.)* Are you hurt? Let me help you. Sit here.

Francesca: These damn shoes. Oh, my knee . . .

Sam: *(examines her knee)* Your knee's fine. But I think your dignity is hurt. Why are you so angry?

Francesca: More than my dignity! And my anger is none of your business.

Sam: Maybe yes, maybe no. A pretty girl like you shouldn't be so angry. Jenny said being angry puts lines on your face.

Francesca: Who's Jennie?

Sam: My wife. *(Young man approaches and addresses Sam)*

Scott: O. K. if I sit here?

Sam: All of a sudden, I'm getting very popular. Sit, sit.

Francesca: Don't you dare!

Sam: Young lady . . .

122

Scott: Her name is Francesca.

Sam: So you are friends?

Francesca: We're friends.

Scott: We're engaged.

Francesca: We're engaged.

Sam: Is he why you're angry?

Scott: Listen, Franny . . .

Francesca: I don't want to hear anything you have to say! Furthermore . . .

Sam: Children, Children, don't fight!

Francesca: Then tell him to leave. This is our bench.

Sam: Boychick, this is our bench!

Scott: You keep out of this! What happened to your knee?

Francesca: Would you please tell him . . . uh . . .

Sam: Sam.

Francesca: Sam, would you please tell that . . . that creature sitting next to you that we have nothing to say to one another.

Sam: Jenny always said, "When you have nothing to say, it doesn't mean that you have nothing to say, just that at that time you shouldn't say it, because you really have plenty to say."

Scott: Who's Jenny?

Francesca: His wife.

Scott: He a friend of yours?

Sam: What else?

Francesca: I'm never getting married.

Sam: That makes it a very long engagement.

Scott: Your mother would love that, wouldn't she, Franny?

Francesca: Leave my mother out of this!

Scott: Wish we could.

Sam: You have something against mothers?

Francesca: Not mothers, Sam. My Mother!

Sam: You don't like her mother before she even becomes a mother-in-law?

Scott: Her mother doesn't like me because I'm going to be her son-in-law.

Francesca: Oh, no you're not!

Sam: Francesca, be quiet a minute. So tell me, Scott. Why doesn't she like you.

Scott: I go to the wrong church.

Sam: Is there such a thing as a wrong church? They're all houses of God.

Scott: Try telling that to her mother.

Sam: I don't know her mother. I only just met you two.

Scott: I thought he was a friend of yours?

Sam: You know, boychick, I sued to think that it was a crime, a sin, if God forbid, a child should marry outside his religion. You know what? It's not such a terrible thing today.

Scott: Try telling that to her mother.

Sam: You'll introduce me, I'll tell her.

Francesca: What made you change?

Sam: Jennie.

Scott: Good! Let's introduce Jennie to her mother.

Sam: Oy, I wish I could. My Jennie's gone.

Scott: Oh, I'm sorry.

Sam: I'm sorry, too. So, you ready to switch seats with me?

Francesca: Don't bother. I'm leaving.

Sam: Franny, Sit! Don't be in such a hurry to get no place. The way I see it is that you love him and he loves you. Now, the problem is . . . what is the problem?

Francesca: He doesn't go to church.

Scott: Her mother called me a pagan. A Pagan! For heaven's sakes, the only idol I worship is Francesca! I just don't want all that religious mumbo-jumbo at our wedding.

Francesca: It's my wedding too. And it's my mother. I can't be happy if she is so upset.

Sam: Upset? Believe me, she doesn't know what upset is. Let me tell you. It was 1942 and we were fighting a war. The whole world was meshuggah – crazy. Altho' to tell the truth, I think it's crazier today. Anyhow, my son got drafted. He comes home one day, married! To a Catholic! He was dead! In my eyes, he was dead! You marry a Jewish girl or you are not my son. I told Jennie that I'm sitting shiva – that's in mourning – for him. Oy, my heart was broken . . . broken.

Scott: What happened?

Sam: Jennie says to me, "Sam, Herman is your son. Your flesh and blood. If the King of England can give up his throne for the woman he loves, how can you put your son in the grave when he brings home the woman he loves?"

Francesca: What did you do?

Francesca: What did you do?

Sam: What'd I do? Nothing. Thank God, he came home from the war and they've been married 40 years. What can I tell you?

Francesca: You mean we should elope?

Sam: God forbid! Your mama would hate me and she doesn't even know me! Scott, would it be so terrible, as long as you don't have any religion, to be married by a priest or minister? What would it hurt? *(silence)* You want to switch seats?

Scott: Why not? *(Sam gets up and Scott moves over to Francesca.)*

Sam: *(still standing)* Listen, you two. My daughter sent me to the store for a dozen eggs 2 hours ago. If she needed them for a recipe . . . oy . . . am I in trouble. Reconsider, you two, fighting's only good if it leads somewhere. *(Sam exits as Scott and Francesca stare after him.)*

FINIS

SCENE THREE

Another afternoon. An obviously pregnant teenager is sitting on the park bench. Sam approaches.

Sam: Good afternoon, young lady. Mind if I join you?

Roxanne: You got a thing for pregnant teeny boppers?

Sam: Nu? Oy, today's world. So I'll take another bench.

Roxanne: Hey, sit down. What do I care.

Sam: *(Holding out a bag)* You like pistachio nuts?

Roxanne: Yeah. *(takes some)* That's fun. *(Silence for a moment)*

Sam: So I'm a comedian. Why aren't you laughing?

Roxanne: What do I have to laugh about?

Sam: Don't ask me! I thought you might like some pistachio nuts and you say that's funny.

Roxanne: Man, are you a weirdo. What's funny is that I love pistachio nuts but I hate pistachio ice-cream.

Sam: Like I should know. So – when are you expecting?

Roxanne: In a couple of weeks.

Sam: That soon?

Roxanne: It's not too soon for me.

Sam: My name is Sam. And yours?

Roxanne: My what?

Sam: Your name? Mine is Sam.

Roxanne: I heard you . . . Rocky.

Sam: Rocky? A very nice name . . . what kind of a name is Rocky?

Roxanne: What kind of a name is Sam?

Sam: Ah . . . a noble name. Samuel. There was once a gret Hebrew Prophet, Samuel.

Roxanne: Is that what you are? A Hebe?

Sam: I prefer Hebrew, but if you like Hebe, that's alright.

Roxanne: Roxanne.

Sam: Roxanne?

Roxanne: That's my name.

Sam: Of course. You look more like a beautful Roxanne than a prizefighter.

Roxanne: Beautiful? She-it!

Sam: Everytime Jenny used to see a young woman who was expecting, she'd say, "Look, Sam, did you ever see anything so beautiful?"

Roxanne: Good for Jenny. You can tell her that a couple of weeks, I'm gonna dump this beauty and good riddance!

Sam: What kind of talk is that!

Roxanne: Hey, man . . .

Sam: Sam!

Roxanne: Well, cool it, Sam. You sat here? O. K. You're better than a lotta creeps around here, but don't you get on my back!

Sam: Dump! Cool it! Don't get on my back! It tell you Roxanne, if I was coming to this country today and had to learn this new language, I'd be in terrible trouble. They teach you this high school?

Roxanne: Never went to high school.

Sam: Listen. It's alright. Some things you don't have to go to school for.

Roxanne: Tell me about it!

Sam: Excuse me. I didn't mean anything personal.

Roxanne: Forget it!

Sam: How times change. When Jennie was in a family way, the clothes were so different.

Roxanne: "A family way". And I talk fun? You mean these jeans? They're maternity jeans, ya know. Cut out in the middle with a string around the waist. Wanna see?

Sam: No, no. I believe you. She used to wear those big loose dresses, God forbid, you should tie anything around the waist. That might mean the baby's cord would twist around its neck.

Roxanne: Hey, I don't know nothin about havin a kid, but how can something you wear on the outside of anything to the kid on the inside?

Sam: What are you asking me? I'm a doctor? So tell me. What about the papa?

Roxanne: My papa? Never knew the creep! I hope he's dead wherever he is.

Sam: Not your papa. The baby's papa. *(Silence)* Ah, I see.

Roxanne: You don't see nothin! You didn't see this crummy bench was occupied, and you didn't see that I didn't want your crummy company, and I didn't want to get knocked up, and bring a kid into this crummy world, and I don't want to marry the creep who knocked up up and *(starts to cry and Sam reaches out to pat her head and she pushs his hand away)* and I don't need any of your crummy sympathy!

Sam: Why should I give you sympathy? You've giving yourself enough for both of us.

Roxanne: Why shouldn't I feel sorry for myself?

Sam: Jenny used to say to the children, "Alright. Feel sorry for yourself for ten minutes. Then, enough!" She was right. What does it get you?

Roxanne: It makes me feel better?

Sam: That's how you feel better?

Roxanne: *(stepping on his line)* Bug off, Sam. Leave me alone!

Sam: Bug off. Another one. Oy, am I getting an English lesson today. Aha! I think I see a smile.

Roxanne: Sam . . . they want me to give the baby away.

Sam: Who?

Roxanne: Everyone.

Same: And you?

Roxanne: Of course! What am I gonna do with a kid? Who needs it? I shoulda had an abortion.

Sam: Why didn't you?

Roxanne: I dunno.

Sam: We came over from Russia and lived in a one room in a tenement. I just made enough to feed Jennie and me and our son. So one day, Jennie tells me she's pregnant. So I said, "What do we need it for? I can't make ends meet, now." And Jennie said, "Sam, God'll provide!" So I said, "What's the address, I'll send God all the doctor bills!" Oy, such a long time ago.

Roxanne: Jennie your wife?

Sam: She was. She's gone.

Roxanne: Jees, Sam. Why dincha tell me?

Sam: It's alright, it's alright.

Roxanne: Did you have the kid?

Sam: What else? Who would I live with now if we didn't have her. So?

Roxanne: I dunno, Sam. I think I'm gonna give it up. But, Sam, suppose 15 years from now, the kid says, "Why didn't my mama want me?"

Sam: If the baby is lucky, she'll have a mama who'll tell her, "Because you real mama loved you too much!"

Roxanee: Will that be the truth, Sam? I gotta go . . . *(gets up and starts to walk away.)* Sam . . . I'm scared . . . *(walks away)*

Sam: Oy, maidele, aren't we all?

FINIS

SCENE FOUR

Woman in her 70's approaches the bench where Sam is sitting.

Sophie: It's such a beautiful day. Would you like some company?

Sam: I wouldn't mind.

Sophie: I've seen you here before.

Sam: You might call this bench my home away from home.

Sophie: You live near here?

Sam: Not far. And you?

Sophie: 5410 Belvedere Avenue, Apt. 26.

Sam: You always give your complete address to strangers?

Sophie: You're not strange I told you. I see you here a lot.

Sam: Since I'm not so strange, I'll tell you my name. It's Sam.

Sophie: How do you do. I'm Sophie Berger. You go to the Temple here?

Sam: You asking me if I'm Jewish?

Sophie: Well, it's nice to start off with something in common.

Sam: So we've got Jewish in common.

Sophie: You live alone?

Sam: You asking me if there's a "Mrs"?

Sophie: Well . . .

Sam: It's alright. There used to be. Her name was Jennie. So tell me, do we have that in common, too?

128

Sophie: His name was Jake. Two years ago he had a stroke and died. I'll tell you, Sam, sometimes, I forget what he looked like. Know what I mean?

Sam: What then? Of course I know. You remember a name, a time, but sometimes you try so hard to find the face and it gets mixed up. Do you try to remember the face in the coffin? or when she was sick? Or do you try to remember what she looked like when you both stood under the Huppa and the rabbi joined you together. It's hard. It's very hard.

Sophie: And I feel guilty when I can't remember. Guilty. But why should I feel guilty? I was a good wife . . . 43 years I was a wife to Jake.

Sam: Why do we feel guilty? Because we're here, that's why. Tell me, Sophie, would you rather be up there *(points to sky)* and let Jake be here feeling guilty about not remembering your face?

Sophie: What kind of a question is that?

Sam: It's a nice question . . . as questions go.

Sophie: You live alone?

Sam: With my daughter.

Sophie: My daughter lives in Paris. Hoo-hah!

Sam: Paris? That's very nice. She didn't want you with her?

Sophie: Sure she wanted me with her . . . I think she wanted me with her. To tell you the truth, I think she was relieved when I told her "no".

Sam: You didn't want to see the world?

Sophie: Sam, look at me. I belong in Paris, France? I belong here. This is my home. I remember coming over from Poland. I was just a little girl. The boat was so filled with people . . . I remember I was sick from the rocking and my mama held me and said, "No more, Sophele. No more will we go through this. We're going to a wonderful country and you'll never have to leave it. You'll have a wonderful life in our new home." . . . This is my home. Like yesterday. I can remember it like yesterday, so why can't I remember my Jake's face?

Sam: You just had the one daughter?

Sophie: I have a son in California. He wants me, too. But a daughter-in-law is not a daughter. Believe me, Pamela is a wonderful girl, but she's not a daughter. On the other hand, she's better than a nursing home with old people.

Sam: Nursing home? You've got years ahead of you before you even think of a nursing home.

Sophie: At least in a nursing home you have company.

Sam: Such company you shouldn't know from.

Sophie: Sam, I'm lonely. Aren't you lonely sometimes?

Sam: Everybody is lonely, sometimes. You think it's just for old people? Believe me, Sophie, I see plenty of young people who are lonely. But you? You're not lonely.

Sophie: What do you mean, I'm not lonely? I'm telling you I'm lonely. Who should know better than me?

Sam: No. You made a mistake. You are alone. There's a difference. With your looks and personality, you should never be alone.

Sophie: You think I'm attractive?

Sam: Would I say it if I didn't believe it?

Sophie: I've got a nice personality?

Sam: Listen, I wouldn't be surprised if sometime soon you met up with someone who wanted nice female companionship.

Sophie: To tell you the truth, that's exactly what I had in mind. We wouldn't have to get married, or anything. Besides, it might affect our Social Security. But why can't two people live together and give each other comfort in our senior years?

Sam: I understand a lot of people are doing it. Cuts down expenses, too.

Sophie: It's so hard to cook for one person. How can you make just a small pot of chicken soup? You have to get a whole fowl to make it good. So what happens? I look around for someone who is sick so I can bring them the chicken soup, but I keep a little for myself. How's your health?

Sam: Thank God. But when it's not so good, Jennie taught my daughter how to make a good chicken soup.

Sophie: That's nice. Can you see my daughter making chicken soup in Paris, France?

Sam: Why not? Frenchmen don't get sick?

Sophie: Sam, be honest with me. You like living with your daughter?

Sam: Sometimes it's good. Sometimes it's not so good.

Sophie: I don't know. Sometimes when I'm alone, I think maybe, just maybe, I'll move out to California with my son. But, Sam, I relly don't think he wants me. He calls me regular, every Sunday. Like clockwork. Every Sunday, he says, "Mom? How you doing?" And I say, "Fine, Howard. And how is Pamela and the children?" And he says, "Terrific, Mom and they all send their love. Wait, the kids want to say "Hello." And the kids get on the phone and say, "Hello, grandma. How are you? We have to go now. Bye." And Pamela gets on the phone and says, "Hello, Mother, how are you?" And I say, "I'm fine, thank you." And she says, "Keep up the good work." And then Howard gets on the phone and says, "What do you say, Mom. Are you ready to move out here with us?" And I say, "Thank you, Howard, but how could I leave my apartment and my friends?" And he says, "I understand, mom." And I say, "This call is costing you a lot of money". And he says, "Don't worry about it.

If you change your mind, let me know." And we say goodbye. Every Sunday, like clockwork! Why doesn't he want me, Sam? I changed his diapers! I wiped his nose! I gave birth to him. Why doesn't he want me?

Sam: He wants you, Sophie. But he's involved with his own family and his own day to day living. It's not like it was years ago. Today, an older parent is like someone from a foreign planet, they think. We're from a different time. We don't think like them and we don't act like them and we want them to think and act like us! Have you ever found a person who could keep his mouth shut?

Sophie: I swear, God should cut out my tongue, if I would open my mouth!

Sam: Not to open your mouth would be like you are dead. And you look very much alive to me.

Sophie: But you live with your daughter.

Sam: And my daughter treats me like one of her children. I let her. And I go my own way. I don't know what will be when they get old. We won't be here, but I think it will be better for them. They're learning how to be more independent. They won't be put out to pasture like us.

Sophie: Speaking of pasture, I'm thinking of going down to Florida. Not St. Petersburg, cause I hear that's for older people.

Sam: Miami?

Sophie: Ft. Lauderdale. There's a much younger crowd there. Do you ever go south?

Sam: I used to go with Jennie. Now I stay put.

Sophie: I'm not going for a couple of months. Maybe I could cook some chicken soup for you and you wouldn't have to be sick.

Sam: Sophie Berger . . . 5410 Belvedere Ave., Apt. 26

Sophie: That's some mind you have. Come sometimes and we'll show my son and your daughter that we're not senile, yet.

Sam: That's some invitation.

Sophie: Your daughter expects you home for supper tonight?

Sam: What else?

Sophie: So maybe you'll come and take potluck with me?

Sam: I thank you, Sophie. But tonight is my grandchild's birthday and I must be getting home. I was "out of the way" long enough.

Sophie: But I'll hear from you? You really have the knack for making me feel good.

Sam: (Gets ups, starts to walk away) Why not? (exits)

BLACKOUT

SCENE FIVE

A well-dressed young woman around 30 is sitting on bench. A "bag lady" comes along and starts rummaging through a trash basket nearby.

Anne: Excuse me . . . excuse me . . .

Rosie: Me? You talking to me?

Anne: Yes. Do you come here often?

Rosie: You from welfare?

Anne: I'm not from any agency. I just want to talk to you for a few minutes.

Rosie: I ain't got nothing to say.

Anne: Please. Maybe you can help me.

Rosie: I can't help you, lady.

Anne: Please. Just answer one question and then, maybe, there won't be anymore. Do you come here often?

Rosie: And if I do?

Anne: Won't you sit down, just for a moment. *(Rosie sits.)* I'm looking for someone and I think maybe you can help. I've been coming here for a week, now, and I've talked to so many people. *(starts to cry)* I'm sorry.

Rosie: *(pulls out a dirty rag)* Here, take this.

Anne: No, thank you. I have one. I'm sorry. Thought I was over tears.

Rosie: So what do you want to ask?

Anne: I'm looking for an elderly gentleman . . . about 79-80, 81.

Rosie: What's his name?

Anne: I don't know.

Rosie: And people call me looney?

Anne: I know. It sounds crazy.

Rosie: What do you want him for?

Anne: My husband died a month ago. He made me promise to seek out this man and thank him for making our time together so precious. You ever been married?

Rosie: Nah. Never had the stomach for it.

Anne: Oh.

Rosie: Hey, don't feel sorry. I ain't got any regrets. I didn't always look like this. Wait a minute. *(rummages through one of her bags)* Here. Look at this. *(shows a photo)*

Anne: You're the blond?

Rosie: Surprised, aincha? I was some looker.

Anne: What a handsome man.

Rosie: Yeah. We sure had some good times. (*looks at photo*) That was taken at that fountain in Italy that you throw in the money.

Anne: The Trevi Fountain, in Rome?

Rosie: Yeah, that's it. Let's see. That was around '58. I traveled to Europe with him that whole year. Ha, ha. I was his "secretary."

Anne: You're a secretary?

Rosie: Of course not. I was a gentleman's escort for an evening, week or whatever. Listen, I had a clientele that would knock your eyes out. And I got big bucks. Had plenty of fun, too.

Anne: What happened?

Rosie: I don't want to talk about it. What did your husband die from?

Anne: Cancer.

Rosie: Stinking disease. But I beat it.

Anne: You had cancer?

Rosie: Sure. Breast. Kills my line of work. Used up all my money, too. Stinking disease.

Anne: No hospitalization?

Rosie: Ha! You only get that with a single employer.

Anne: Oh. Yes, of course. Tell me, why do you carry those bags with you? Can't you leave them in your home?

Rosie: Home? Listen, lady. These bags are my home. They are my whole life. If I left them in my room, some broken down junkie would break in and cart them away before you could holler, "cops." You can't trust no one these days.

Anne: I do wish I could have found Lloyd's friend. Someone must know who I'm talking about.

Rosie: You didn't exactly have a picture of him, you know. Not even a first name.

Anne: No. Lloyd used to call him St. Francis.

Rosie: No saints in this park. That's for sure.

Anne: Listen, I don't want to insult you, but you have spent time with me. Would you have a dinner treat on me? (*takes a bill out of her purse*)

Rosie: (*snatches it*) That's mighty nice of you. I don't go begging, you know. But my welfare check doesn't come in till the end of the month.

Anne: Guess I'll be going. (*get up to leave*) This man was Jewish. Would that help?

Rosie: Naw. Could be anyone. Sorry, lady. (*Anne starts to heave.*) Hey, lady, wait a minute. Would he have had a wife, Jenny, who died?

Anne: *(running back)* Yes. Yes, he did. You know him? You know who I'm talking about?

Rosie: I thought . . . but no. It couldn't be Sam.

Anne: Sam?

Rosie: He used to be a regular here after his wife died. Nice old man. Very lonely without his wife.

Anne: That's him. Do you have any idea where he lives?

Rosie: Doesn't make any difference any more. I'm telling you, it couldn't be Sam.

Anne: For heaven's sake, why not?

Rosie: Because Sam died two years ago!

BLACKOUT

It Hardly Matters Now

by Roger Cornish

It Hardly Matters Now

by Roger Cornish

Cast List
Herb   May
Carrie

It Hardly Matters Now

by Roger Cornish

At Rise: This middle class living room belongs to Herb and Carrie. It's comfortable, well appointed, but in no way distinguished. Nor is there anything about it to suggest that its owners are in their retirement years. Nothing, that is, unless it is a quality of order seldom found in homes with small children or adults still caught up in the rat race.

At curtain, Herb, a fine-looking man in his later sixties, is on the phone. He has had it with the party on the other end.

Herb: No, that won't be just as acceptable. I paid for cedar – I want cedar . . . Sure it will, but cedar will last twice as long. (*Carrie, a cheerful-looking woman of Herb's age, sails in. She's dressed for town, whence they recently returned, and she bears a tray of sparkling martini glasses.*)

Herb: . . . Look, I'm not going to waste my time arguing with you – I've got company. Either do it the way we agreed or forget it. And get your damn pine out of my yard! (*He slams the receiver into its cradle, eliciting from Carrie a mock shudder indicating she's seen this temper before.*)

Carrie: Well, that oughta hold him!

Herb: Damn straight! (*They meet at the bar, where Herb begins to mix martinis with a vengeance, slamming ice cubes into the crystal pitcher.*)

Carrie: Hey, don't bruise the ice.

Herb: Can you believe that guy – trying to slip me pine for cedar? Me, an engineer!

Carrie: That bad, huh?

Herb: You know how long pine is good for? Ten years from now we'd have to replace the whole deck.

Carrie: Oh well, ten years . . .

Herb: Now don't you start, dammit . . .

Carrie: Hey, remember me – your wife, the innocent bystander?

Herb: That's just what he was thinking – though he wouldn't dare say it – "what the hell, at their age it doesn't have to last forever."

Carrie: (*With rueful good humor*) Well, does it?

137

Herb: That's not the point! Where does it say I should only eat off paper plates because I'm over sixty-five?

Carrie: Hold it . . . *(She pantomimes correcting a shopping list.)* . . . cross off . . . paper plates!

Herb: And stop buying this cheap gin!

Carrie: *(As before)* Right. How do you spell Tan–que–ray?

Herb *(Giving in)* Mit an umlaut over da Q. Ok, I'll shut up.

Carrie: And give me my martini?

Herb: Let's wait for May. Where is she?

Carrie: Making tinkle. She'll be right along.

Herb: *(With a nod toward their off-stage guest)* What do you think?

Carrie: She's certainly changed.

Herb: Forty-four years – haven't we all?

Carrie: Oh, I know, but she was so . . . so put together – always a pleasure to look at.

Herb: She still is.

Carrie: Ever the gentlemen – still gallant.

Herb: Lord, do you realize I dated May before I dated you?

Carrie: Before and during – how you used to pontificate about your dating style! *(In a deep, pretentious voice)* "A real go-getter plays the field till he's at least thirty."

Herb: I swore I'd be making five thousand a year before I married.

Carrie: Young man with big ideas.

Herb: And not getting married meant something then, too.

Carrie: Didn't I know it? Maybe you were ready to wait that long, but I certainly wasn't.

Herb: Yes, tell me about it – you and May and that famous flip.

Carrie: Flip?

Herb: *(Pouring)* How you flipped a silver dollar to see which one of you would marry me.

Carrie: *(A bit cross)* Oh, that old joke. You know that never happened – I made that up.

Herb: I know, but it could have happened – you girls were crazy enough.

Carrie: Not with marriage, for heaven's sake! *(May's voice is heard a moment before she rushes in.)*

May: Carrie, your house is absolute bliss! *(May is of an age with Carrie and Herb. A bit more high style than Carrie, she wears a fashionable traveling suit.)*

Carrie: Oh, I'm just thrilled to hear you say that.

May: And the garden! It's like Versailles. Even those rose bushes are all the same height.

Herb: Of course. I trained them.

May: Trained them?

Carrie: Oh, you should see him – he's so cute with his hedge clippers and his little yardstick.

Herb: *(Offering)* Martini?

May: *(Accepting)* Por favor.

Herb: *(Serving Carrie, who takes a greedy sip)* Precisely three and a half to one.

May: God, where were you when I had a schizoid Romanian zither player in charge of my production line – talk about organization!

Herb: *(Lifting his glass)* To old times. *(They all drink.)*

May: To next season.

Carrie: Oh, I can't believe you're really here!

May: There were a few times – trying to gas my rent-a-car in Budapest, for instance – I wondered if I'd make it myself.

Carrie: Oh, if you hadn't. I'd have never forgiven you. After forty-four years you couldn't miss us . . .

May: *(Toasting them)* I saved the best for last.

Carrie: *(Hugging her enthusiastically)* Oh, you did, didn't you!

May: Besides, the time to visit old friends is *after* you've spent all your money in Holiday Inns.

Herb: That'll be a buck and a half for the martini.

May: Don't I even get wholesale?

Carrie: *(giggling)* Oh, stop —

May: Didn't she always say that?

Herb: Still does.

Carrie: Oh, stop! Tell us about your trip . . .

May: You mean my valedictory from Smart Set Dresses, my retirement retreat?

Carrie: Oh, yes, the places, the ships, the trains – to just go – the day you retired. How could you?

May: Simple. I took a look at the bottom line – the one where it says: no husband, no job, no plans – and I decided to go on the road. I rented the condominium for a year, hailed a cab, and this is this is the first time I've stood still since. Places? My dear . . .

Carrie: Oh, it sounds so exciting!

May: I took a gigolo to dinner in Puerto Vallarta; I was taken to dinner in Dublin; and in Paris – I was just taken.

Herb: That doesn't sound so good . . .

Carrie: It sounds wonderful!

May: It was wonderful. And spas – health resorts – Carrie, I've had my kneecaps massaged with reindeer glands, my elbows soaked in the saliva of baby pussycats, and if ever I told you what they do with sheep testicles . . .

Carrie: Oh, stop –

Herb: Well, it must be good, because you look gorgeous.

May: One peek at the inside of my elbow and you'd go mad.

Herb: Ah, but I've seen the inside of your elbow.

May: Forty years ago? Kid stuff!

Carrie: Oh, stop! You haven't changed a bit. She hasn't, has she . . .

May: Well, I can't play the piano anymore.

Carrie: You never could!

May: Then I haven't changed, have I?

Carrie: See? She's still the craziest. Oh, I'm having a wonderful time! Herb, make her promise to stay.

Herb: She knows she's welcome.

Carrie: Oh, for heaven's sake! *(To May)* You've got to stay, at least a month. *(To Herb)* And make us another cocktail. *(Herb begins to mix a small dividend.)*

May: A month? Hm. Well, what's the male situation around here?

Carrie: Mail?

May: No, – male.

Carrie: Oh, male!

Herb: What's this – man hunting?

May: Darn right. Why do you think I logged all those miles and spent money like a perfect fool? Now, I'm back, fresh and sassy – retooled for the new season – I'm going to get married again.

Carrie: Wonderful!

Herb: Hm – that'll make what – three?

May: Four, but who counts? Besides, the last divorce was a mistake.

Carrie: Oh, then you could marry him again . . .

May: Too late – died.

Carrie: Oh, I'm sorry.

May: That was the mistake. If I'd stayed married to him, I would have inherited "Smart Set" dresses and they couldn't have retired me – I'd have retired them.

Carrie: But I thought you were having a grand time being retired . . .

May: I cope – but it's a long season.

Herb: The longest. (*Herb pours a small martini for Carrie. May shakes her head no.*)

Carrie: Oh, I love Herb being retired – he keeps things so interesting – just like you did when we were in school.

May: I did, didn't I? And the times we had . . .

Herb: The trouble you two got into – smoking cigarettes, reading "Tropic of Cancer," missing curfews . . .

Carrie: Ten o'clock Friday nights! Did we really grow up in an age like that?

Herb: Some did, but not you and May. Rules were for other people, and woe betide the college man who tried to make you act like Betty Coeds.

May: You should know; you dated both of us.

Herb: Boy, was I a glutton for punishment.

Carrie: Oh, you were a conceited big-man-on-campus. (*To May*) Remember him? Phi Beta Kappa and corncob pipe. There wasn't one thing an intelligent person could stand about you. But you did have good taste in women.

Herb: Someone had to save the two of you from becoming lost ladies.

Carrie: Oh, the ego!

Herb: You needed a smart man to straighten you out.

Carrie: Really? I seem to remember we straightened you out a few times. Remember the night you showed up for a date with me and we made you believe you'd asked May out instead?

Herb: I still don't know how I fell for that one.

Carrie: You looked a perfect fool. Me in my curlers and face cream. May dressed to the nines . . .

May: (*Simpering*) Why, Herbie, did oo forget Maysie-Waysie?

Carrie: . . . and a dozen sorority sisters watching you try to act as if you hadn't just tried to pin camelias on my bathrobe. Wait! I have a picture . . . (*She hurries out.*)

Herb: I couldn't for the life of me understand what was going on. You two were such devils.

May: (*Patting his hand*) We did it for love.

Herb: Yes, you were terrific girls . . . full of adventure. Thank heaven I got smart enough to marry one of you.

May: Smart enough? Aren't you forgetting something?

Herb: What?

May: *(Searching her handbag)* This.

Herb: What is it?

May: Oh, I forgot – you've never actually seen it. Look. *(She hands him a large silver coin at the end of a chain.)*

Herb: A silver dollar?

May: Of course. Remember? She got you; I got the dollar. *(Carrie returns, waving an old snapshot.)*

Carrie: I found it . . . *(May seizes the silver dollar from Herb and extends it toward Carrie.)*

May: Remember this?

Herb: Wait a minute . . . *(Moving rapidly, he retrieves the coin.)*

Herb: Let me have that.

Carrie: *(Oblivious)* Look at this – can you believe we looked . . .

Herb: Never mind that! What the hell is this?

May: I told you – *(The coin thrust under her nose, Carrie suddenly understands)*

Carrie: May, don't . . .

Herb: You be quiet!

May: Herb!

Herb: *(To May, carefully)* Let's get this straight. This is the silver dollar . . .

May: *(Puzzled)* Yes . . .

May: *(To Carrie)* Have I said something . . .?

Carrie: Herb, we'll talk about it later . . .

Herb: I'm talking to May! The silver dollar – worth almost a dime today.

Herb: *(Turning on Carrie)* You . . . *(Unable to articulate, he sputters.)* . . . you . . . . I . . . it's true, you . . . *(Herb sinks heavily into a chair)*

Carrie: Herb . . .

May: Is he all right?

Carrie: I don't know what to say . . .

Herb: *(Rising)* Just don't say anything – not anything. I don't want to hear it. *(Throwing down the coin. Herb rushes out.)*

May: I don't understand . . .

Carrie: *(Picking up the coin)* He didn't know.

May: Of course he knew – you mentioned it a dozen times in your letters.

Carrie: No, he only knew it as a joke.

May: What?
Carrie: The first time I ever mentioned it – we were just kids, and I was furious at him about something – he'd really hurt me – but he took it as a joke, a crazy story. Then I realized it was better that way, so I let well enough alone, and it's been a joke ever since. We fool around; I say, "I won you on a bet," and he always laughs.

May: Carrie, I could cut my tongue out. I'm so sorry . . .

Carrie: *(Slapping the coin down on a table)* Oh, what are we fussing about? *(She empties the martini shaker into her glass.)* It was forty-four years ago.

May: God, remember that night?

Carrie: That morning, you mean – it was almost dawn.

May: And cold . . . the wind ripped through our room . . . windows wide open so nobody could smell us smoking.

Carrie: At five A.M.!

May: Lucky Strikes . . . without filters, God!

Carrie: You said it first; "One of us has to marry Herbert."

May: No, no, you said that.

Carrie: No, I said "The other one has to go to New York City . . . we always said it like that . . . New York City . . . and live in Greenwich Village!"

May: No, that's what I said.

Carrie: Well, whatever . . . I wonder if I would have had the nerve to go to the city by myself and make a career.

May: What's the difference? We flipped a coin, and here you are. And there I went.

Carrie: *(Eating the olive from her martini)* May . . .

May: Yah?

Carrie: That was the luckiest day of my life.

May: Listen, do you want me to talk to him?

Carrie: *(Suddenly cheerful)* Oh, Lord, no! It's all silliness. We're senior citizens, for heaven's sake . . . how could it matter now?

May: Forty-four years and boom! I told you I couldn't keep a secret.

Carrie: *(Giggling)* Blabbermouth! *(Herb walks stonily back into the room.)*

Carrie: Well, she certainly is a blabbermouth, isn't she . . .?

Herb: May, would you leave us alone, please?

Carrie: Oh, Herb, you can't still be mad?

Herb: May . . .

Carrie: No, let her stay. Don't spoil everything . . .

143

Herb: It's already spoiled.

May: I think I'd like to lie down anyway – I'm feeling a bit tired.

Carrie: No, you don't need . . .

Herb: Let her go. *(May exits.)* What am I going to do about this?

Carrie: I don't know about you, but I want another drink.

Herb: Not now. I want this settled.

Carrie: What's there to tell? It was crazy . . . it happened. We've had a wonderful marriage.

Herb: Tell me why.

Carrie: Why?

Herb: Why.

Carrie: I guess . . . we wanted to puncture your balloon.

Herb: My what?

Carrie: Your balloon. That big gassy thing you floated around in – all blown up with success and rectitude, prizes and simpering sorority girls. We decided to let the air out of your bag.

Herb: That's what you thought of me – a gas bag?

Carrie: Oh, but we adored you – just like all the others. We just couldn't stand your being so darn perfect. I suppose we were reading Dorothy Parker.

Herb: But marriage?

Carrie: It seemed a funny idea at the time . . .

Herb: Funny? The white dress, the bridesmaids . . .

Carrie: We thought it was hilarious. Not the wedding, so much – though that was pretty funny – but then the divorce. We figured ninety days. May called it the Co-ed Double . . . the first girl married, plus the first girl divorced. She was going to have a trophy inscribed with my name, and mix champagne punch in it for Homecoming parties. May would have done it, too.

Herb: But you fouled that up – you stayed married.

Carrie: Yes, I never thought I'd like it so much. I was going to go for a career, like May.

Herb: I imagine May was rather disappointed in you.

Carrie: Not at all. That made the joke on me . . . it was even funnier.

Herb: Funnier than my punctured balloon?

Carrie: Oh, but we never managed that, don't you see? All these years and your balloon has never come down . . . only I've been floating up there with you . . . a passenger in the gondola car.

Herb: Well, the balloon's down now.

Carrie: *(With a half smile)* Yes, you do look a bit deflated.

Herb: Are you going to laugh?

Carrie: If you do . . .

Herb: Well, I can't. You've made a fool of me.

Carrie: Forty-four years ago . . .

Herb: It feels like today . . . and it hurts.

Carrie: Herb, I don't know what I'm supposed to say, except I'm sorry and I love you.

Herb: I'm sorry, but that's too easy.

Carrie: What do you want – an annulment?

Herb: You think that's funny? Listen, there's no statute of limitations on the crimes women commit against men.

Carrie: You could forgive me.

Herb: Did you ever forgive me for . . . Miss What's-her-name, in Baltimore?

Carrie: *(With an edge)* Miss Bailey.

Herb: See? You remember her name.

Carrie: We were young then . . . it hurt!

Herb: There it is again. I'm so sold I'm supposed to be invulnerable? Nothing stings anymore?

Carrie: No, it's not that . . .

Herb: I'm not supposed to care if my clothes are out style – who am I trying to impress at my age?

Carrie: Herb, please . . .

Herb: After all, he's neat and clean. *(He grabs the gin bottle.)* And I'm not supposed to worry if you drink too much . . . what the hell, she's over sixty-five!

Carrie: Oh, Herb . . . *(She sinks into a chair, her hand, wanly clutching an empty glass, drooping into her lap.)*

Herb: Well, I do care, and if something's wrong. I want it right. I don't care if I'm a hundred!

Carrie: But what can I do? *(A traveling bag in one hand. May appears in the doorway.)*

May: Nothing, my dear, because he's right. But you could drive me to the airport.

Herb: May, no! I didn't mean . . .

Carrie: *(Speaking over him as she rushes to May)* Oh, please, no. It's just a silly argument, really . . .

May: Shhh. It's been lovely seeing you both, and I adore you both. But, Carrie, we did it, and it's caught up with us . . .

Herb: Listen, May, it's alright . . . I'll calm down. Carrie's right. It's so many years . . .

May: Yes, but it hurts you now, just as it would have then.

Herb: I'll get over it.

May: Of course, and I'll visit again – or you'll visit me – but not right now. I feel I have to pay some price for what I did.

Carrie: Even now?

May: You don't outlive your debts . . . you either pay them or you don't. *(She is heading for the door.)* I'll be out in the car. *(She stops in the doorway.)* Oh, one thing, Carrie . . . when we tossed that coin . . .

Carrie: Yes?

May: I really wanted to be made to take my fling; I wanted to have to New York on my own.

Carrie: You did?

May: And you wanted to be made to get married . . . to marry Herb.

Carrie: Oh, no . . .

May: Oh, yes, my dear, you wanted to be taken care of. The proof is that we both did what the coin told us to do. We could have reneged.

Herb: Then what am I so angry about?

May: Enough. But when we tossed that coin . . . everybody won. *(She exits.)*

Carrie: She's really going . . .

Herb: I'll drive her . . . maybe I can change her mind. *(Herb follows May off. After a moment, Carrie steps over to the bar and hefts the martini pitcher. Then something catches her eye and she puts it down. She stops to the table and picks up the silver dollar and chain. Suddenly she smiles and hurries after them.)*

Carrie: Hey, wait for me . . . I'm not getting left with the dollar!

CURTAIN

Just A Song At Twilight

by Marcia Savin

Just A Song At Twilight

by Marcia Savin

Cast List
He   She

Just A Song At Twilight

by Marcia Savin

A park bench. Winter. A bare-branched tree. A man in his sixties sits on the bench. He wears overcoat, muffler, is bare-headed, most of his hair gone. A thermos bottle beside him, unopened. A woman enters. Also in her sixties. She is unfamiliar with her surroundings. She carries a mover's inventory, which she reads.

He: Did you get all moved in?

She: Oh, you were watching! You wouldn't believe what they wanted to come a few miles.

He: On behalf of the Tenants Organization, let me welcome you to subsidized housing. It's the only good thing about growing old. That, and the bus passes.

She: You're telling me. I don't know how long I could have held out, if the vacancy hadn't come up. Either pay rent, or have heat! Of course, I couldn't help feeling bad, too. I mean, on the one hand, being so relieved to hear that a place had come up here, and on the other, knowing that the only reason one would –

He: I'm sure that Mr. Feldman, wherever he is, would be happy to know that such an attractive person has taken his place.

She: I'm only taking the gentleman's apartment – not his place.

He: Unless you know everything there is to know about the wildlife along the Hudson River Valley, and unless you impart this information at the drop of a 'good morning', you couldn't possibly take Joe Feldman's place.

pause

Have a seat.

She: *(hesitant)* Oh, I should –

He: Unless this air is too sharp for you. I like it myself.

She: Are you kidding? You are looking at someone who loves winter. Whenever there's fresh snow on the ground, I go out for a long walk. Then come back and make a fire. And later, maybe some hot buttered rum . . . I'm going to miss that fireplace.

He: I happen to have a hot drink here.

149

She: Thank you. I'd love it – but I was just stopping for a minute. I've all those boxes to unpack.

He: Do you like hot toddies?

She: Oh I do. I definitely do.

He: It's one of the things I make really well.

She: And I would love one. Another time. Thanks.

He: Look, I know you think I'm an old souse sitting out here in the park sneaking hot toddies –

She: *(uncertain)* Oh, not for a minute!

He: For the past five years I've ben meeting a friend here in the afternoons. And sometimes I'd bring a thermos of coffee. Today I felt like something stronger. Look. I made too much. How can I drink all that myself? And make it back upstairs?

She: Um . . . smell that lemon.

He: After all, how often does an attractive woman move into our building? We have to toast your arrival.

She: Oh, listen to the man. Well . . . a small one. *(sits)* Moving does take a lot out of you.

He: This will put something back in. *(hands her a drink in thermos lid)*

She: Isn't your friend coming down?

He: He died last week.

She: Oh, I'm sorry –

He: Hey, look at that jay. How blue he is. Reminds me of cardinals you see down south. In the middle of winter. This bright red bird would be sitting in a bare bush, with snow all around him. Bright red, bright red against the snow.

She: A gentleman friend of mine died this year. Very sweet man. We used to go dancing. *(pause)* It's terrible. You no sooner die than they're taking your place – *(She's deliberately changing the original 'your' to 'my')* "Somebody elso is taking your place/

Somebody else now shares your embrace . . ."

(can't remember the rest)

He: "two hearts are crying/

two lips are signing/

cause . . ."

Together: "Somebody's tak-ing your pla-a-ce . . ."

She: *(laughs)* Oh, aren't we terrible!

He: I thought the harmony was pretty good.

She: I mean about Mr. Feld – OHHH – he must be the friend –

He: Reluctant as I am to leave this green earth – even this muddy brown one – I know the day will come. And I only hope that I go like Joe Feldman: a swimmer moving peacefully along in the water who suddenly takes a whim to glide down beneath the surface. And that's it.

She: *(toasting; click cups)* May we all go like that. I have friends who can't talk about death.

He: I met a woman in the hall the other day. She said: "We lost Al." I almost said, "Have you looked in the park?" They lost Al! They knew damn well where he was. *(takes out cigar)* I always have my first of the day around the cocktail hour. *(squints at sun)* I'd say it's the cocktail hour, wouldn't you? Do you mind if I smoke?

She: No, I love the smell of cigars. Somebody I used to know smoked them.

He: You know, I think you lied about your age to get in here. You can't be old enough.

She: Oh, I'm old enough. I retired a few months ago. And that lousy company I worked for tried to keep my pension!

He: You'll be the kid of the building.

She: Are all the other men terrible flatterers, too?

He: How can I answer that and win? If I were a flatterer, I'd have a rich wife. And smoke cigars all day.

She: She might not let you! The dear friend of mine who died wanted me to marry him. Oh, for years! I was very fond of him. But after living alone so long, I don't think I could get used to sharing an apartment again. I had a garden, a fireplace . . .

He: Regret leaving it?

She: Me? I never regret anything! It's a waste of time.

He: I have no regrets either. Because I make it a point to forget everything.

She: I remember everything! I may be over sixty, but my head is absolutely clear. I remember everything! I even remember – in spite of your delicious hot toddy – that I must be toddling on up to that apartment. There's no room to walk in there. *(hands cup back; he won't take it)*

He: There won't be after you unpack either. I only go up to sleep.

She: Well, if you get to our age and you haven't learned to adjust, they give you a keeper. Thank you again for the wonderful drink – *(rises)*

He: You remember everything and you regret nothing! You must have led a great life!

She: Oh, I had bad times. Who hasn't? But I don't bother remembering them. I just remember the wonderful times.

He: I thought you said you remembered everything.

She: I remember the bad times, I just don't think about them. *(takes a last swallow)* Nutmeg. There's nutmeg in here.

He: *(proudly displaying it)* Cut my thumb on the grater. Tell me about the wonderful old times.

She: I will. Another day.

He: Do you have any idea how many times I've listened to arguments about the fastest way to get to Times Square?

She: Do you have any idea how much stuff is up there waiting for me? And I threw out almost everything I owned.

He: I see. Your past is too wicked to discuss with strangers.

She: You're not a stranger.

He: Then you've forgotten it.

She: I remember everything that mattered. Everything that mattered.

He: And all the beaux whose hearts you broke?

She: I didn't break any hearts. If I did, they all recovered.

He: That's because they were young. But will I recover? An old man alone in the park with a thermos half full of warmish toddies . . . left to mourn old Joe, his last friend?

She: Listen to the man. You were making fun of him and his wildlife talks.

He: I may kid about Joe but I would give anything to have him tell me how the cardinal and the blue jay keep their colors when everything else is drab and gray. Joe would have liked you and he would have been sorely disappointed to think that you'd rather unpack than share my last drop of toddy. On this beautiful bright day. Joe would have let his boxes stay packed for a week in weather like this.

She: Oh, you must have been the youngest in your family!

He: *(pouring them another drink)* If you read minds, I'm leaving while I'm still safe.

She: No . . .

He: If you read fortunes, I don't want to know mine.

She: There's no trick. The baby always grows up to be a charmer. Boys and girls. But boys are worse. They practice on their mothers and their older sisters –

He: *(laughs in acknowledgement)*

She: When you see a fellow talking his way out of something – he'll turn out to be the youngest in the family, every time. And I'll tell you something else: the older you men get, the more you turn on that old charm.

He: What else have we left?

She: Oh, I'm not complaining. You notice I'm not unpacking boxes.

He: Now I'll do some fortune telling. I think that once upon a time you fell for a youngest son –

She: *(sitting)* That I did. That I did.

He: – who broke your heart and you've been blaming the rest of us innocent, well-meaning, but unfortunately last-born, fellows, ever since.

She: Oh no. Because for one, he didn't break my heart. So I have nothing to blame him for. Or any of you "innocents" either.

He: I've heard, that somewhere West of Burma – and this has been documented – there lives a woman who doesn't blame any man for anything. But I've never seen her myself.

She: Well, you're looking at another one. And we were talking about one particular man who made all the difference to me between being alive and just waiting around the Christmas bonus.

He: A lucky man.

She: It was me who was lucky. I think everyone has one special love that they remember all their life.

He: I remember a dog who bit me. It was in Tucson.

She: I think you're covering up –

He: No. See . . . *(raises pants leg)* . . . the scar above the ankle?

She: Never "one great love"?

He: Oh, several started out to be –

She: You're a cynical man.

He: At least you didn't say "a cynical old man."

She: I think I would have felt I missed something . . . if there hadn't been that one man who just charmed me to pieces.

He: It happens to me all the time. Men, women, dogs. I still remember that cardinal against the snow. Must have been seventeen years ago. So red you couldn't believe it. Just standing in this bush. No leaves left. Snow all around him. In the middle of winter. Just when everything was dying. I wanted to hug him. *(pause)* I'm not cynical. I just think that great loves are probably nice affairs which get great in someone's imagination afterwards. That's all right. I just don't have that kind of imagination.

She: It's not imagination! I remember it all – just as it was.

He: Those wonderful old times? They're always so damn short.

She: Well, the thing itself didn't last very long. But the memory – It's not that I didn't care for others. But not like that. Oh, not like that.

He: I think there's a little more in here.

She: You know, if I don't unpack I won't have a place to sleep –

He: But *(she keeps walking; suddenly she stops and turns)*

She: This morning, waiting for the movers, I stood and looked at everything I owned in the world, packed up. And it didn't fill a corner of the room. But I thought – the memories are invisible. That's why I wouldn't part with mine for any money.

He: How much have you been offered?

She: You! What happened to you to make you such a cynic?

He: If you'd stop being so eager to leave, and wait a minute, I'll help you. You already packed up all that damn stuff this morning. Finish your drink and than I'll help you. I know all about packing.

She: Thanks, but it's a big job –

He: I have nothing else to do. I want to hear about this great love. Having never had anyone myself, I'm curious. I'll bet you only really appreciated this fellow after he was gone?

She: Appreciate him! The very first time I laid eyes on that man – No! . . . not the very first. The first time he was with some friends and they were all clowning around. I thought he was immature. I was eighteen and wore my hair up and wore silk stockings. And I thought I liked serious men. With moustaches. *(amused)* Back in those days, you remember – before the War – serious men who got ahead wore moustaches. Like old Tom Dewey. But this fellow had no moustache and wasn't serious. The second time – it was the second time I saw him. It was summer. And his shirt was open at the throat. I don't know what it was. I just kept looking at his neck.

He: Was there something unusual about it?

She: Yes, but I couldn't tell you now what it was. When I met him – someone introduced us – he thought he was meeting me for the first time. But I had been watching him for I don't know how long. Him and that neck. The Adam's apple. The back of it. I could never get mad at the man just after he'd had a haircut. With that raw and helpless look around the ears. Well, it didn't take us long. There was never anyone like him.

He: I never knew a neck could be so interesting.

She: I guess that sounds silly. It wasn't just his neck. There was a way his arms swung away from his body when he walked. Like he belonged in the world. I've stopped on the street a hundred times since then thinking I saw him. But it was just someone with that walk. With almost that walk. But there was that neck. Oh, when that man pulled his necktie off . . . and loosened his collar . . . Oh, I tell you. I shivered.

He: I've heard that some women like a man's chest.

She: What chest? He was all bones. I'm talking about the man's neck. His throat. Collarbones . . .

He: And I used to stand in front of the mirror flexing my biceps.

She: You really got me started. But I just want you to understand that I didn't start to appreciate this man after he was gone. No sir. I appreciated this man the second time I saw him. And after that I appreciated him when he was awake . . . asleep . . . with me . . . away from me. I appreciated the morning because he was alive in it.

He: I thought feelings like that were just in books.

She: Sometimes he worked nights and in the afternoons I'd watch him sleep. There was a fellow next door who played the sax and I remember listening to the music and watching that man sleep, just drinking him in.

He: *(the mention of the "sax" triggers a memory)* How could you leave him?

She: Oh, I didn't. He left.

He: How could he leave you?

She: Well, the man was a perfectionist. If you know anything about perfectionists –

He: *(thinks ruefully of himself)* They're impossible to live with.

She: They're never satisfied. I don't mean about us – I mean the rest of his life. He couldn't find what he wanted. Some people are too talented. They can't decide. Anyway, he left. We shook hands and said goodbye.

He: You might get me to believe in the great love. Or in the shaking hands and saying goodbye. But not both. I spent the last fifteen years of my working life in the brewery. And there's nothing but talk; of fights, and cheating and beatings – but I've never heard of a love affair that ended with two people shaking hands and saying goodbye.

She: I remember everything. I have a perfect memory. You can ask my daughter about my memory. Except she's out in California. We shook hands and said goodbye. What else was there to do? I could see the man was miserable. I knew he didn't want to hurt me. When someone wants to go, that's the time to put out your hand and say goodbye.

He: When someone wants to go, in my experience, is the time when everyone starts hanging on for dear life.

She: I don't know about your experience. I'm not everyone. *(starts to leave)*

He: *(following)* My dear lady, I'm only too aware of that. You think I'd share my hot toddy with just any women who happens to appear in the park? I think you're amazing, in fact.

She: *(suddenly turning around to him)* Listen – I've always wanted a garden. Finally, I found this little garden apartment. And the first thing I did, before I even put up curtains, was to start planting –

He: I've got a fern. But it hasn't been doing too well lately.

She: – no matter how tired I was when I came home from work, I'd go out and get those weeds. Because if I'm going to have a garden. I'm going to have a garden. I'm going to have peppers and lettuce. And three different kinds of tomatoes. And I'm going to have cucumbers and onions and carrots –

He: I thought we were talking about people saying goodbye –

She: We are. Just wait. And not just vegetables. My mother used to grow sweet peas on our fire escape and I never forgot the smell of them in August. So I had sweet peas growing on the fences, the walls . . . all colors. From white to purple. And oh, I had a cherry tree. The day the blossoms come out you can't even hate the company that's trying to swindle you out of your pension. The blossoms could break your heart – they last so short a time.

He: Like great love?

She: No, that lasts forever. That's what I'm explaining. That was my garden. But the rent kept going up and so now I'm here. Where the subsidy allows for two small rooms and maybe two tomato plants and three petunias on your window sill. But that's all right. That's all right with me. I won't have anything. Because if I'm going to have a garden, I'm –

He: – going to have a garden.

She: And if I'm going to have a marriage, I'm not going to hang onto a corpse.

He: You married this man – this man you felt that way about? You married him – and still you just shook hands and said goodbye? You're amazing.

She: I'm not amazing. I'm fussy. Is there any more in there?

He: A few drops. No. You're amazing. Married, and you look at it like that!

She: *(saxophone in distance plays "Blueberry Hill," "Sweet Lorraine," "Honeysuckle Rose")* Isn't that music? Or am I just back in the past?

He: That's old Ben. Usually starts when the sun goes down. He's damn good. Especially after a bottle. Always stands on the corner in front of the burger place.

She: Oh, that music takes me back! Do you dance?

He: Oh, I haven't for years! Now, why didn't I ever meet a sensible lady like you?

She: Sensible? If I was sensible, I'd be upstairs unpacking. Instead of sitting out here getting drunk with you. And old Ben.

He: *(rises)* Come on.

She: *(rising)* Oh, we're finally going?

He: We're going to dance. I can't dance, but I'll show you no one's drunk.

She: The people in the building will think I'm crazy.

He: They're all huddled by their radiators waiting for spring. *(They do the fox trot.)*

She: What do you mean you "can't dance"?

He: Oh sometimes I'm lucky enough to find a partner whose irresistible force can overcome my immovable body.

She: You don't talk like someone in a brewery.

He: Sometimes you need a job. You wouldn't have let him go easily, I'll bet, if there had been a child.

She: Who said there wasn't?

He: You couldn't have felt that way about a man who left you with a child!

She: And I'm saying that's exactly how I felt. I had a baby and I was crazy about her. In fact, it would have been much worse without her.

He: You didn't think the man owed you something?

She: Mike never owed me anything. *(He knows her now but is afraid to tell her.)*

He: Not even money?

She: Money? I didn't know we were talking about money. Sure, he sent money. When he had it. I'd get money orders from all over. Los Angeles. Chicago. Even Paris.

He: And you didn't expect anything else from him?

She: When a man is hundreds of miles away, there isn't anything he can do for you. And I didn't want anything from him. It was over.

He: But he left you with all the problems while he went off to be a great – whatever.

She: Musician. But he didn't go off to be one. He was one. *(Guilty and uncomfortable he turns away.)* Mike could sit down to that little white upright and pick out any tune. Anything. All by ear. In fact, he even had a little band. They played around the neighborhoods. The others wanted to try and make it big, but Mike was scared.

He: Scared?

She: The man was a perfectionist. Said they weren't good enough.

He: He was probably right.

She: He didn't try to find out! They could have been famous, I know it. Because he was brilliant. And music was just one of his talents. He read books all the time. But he was a very restless man.

He: *(takes her hand to dance again)* I think it's you who is not like anyone else.

She: Oh, listen to you! Do you "dip"?

He: Well, it's been a hell of a long time, but I'm certainly willing to try! *(they dip, as in a tango, laughing)*

She: *(they wrench their backs and she falls back onto the bench)* Oh, I tell you, my memories took me over some rough times. The worse was when I lost my job. Not with the lousy company I worked for just this year. This was another lousy company. Lousier, in fact. They fired me without warning, without an extra pay check – and I had just had big medical expenses, and I'll tell you – it was rough!

He: *(uncomfortable at this, tries to distract her)* I thought you only remembered the good times!

She: Well, this was so bad it was funny. Here I was out of work, with a cold or flu that I couldn't get rid of, so whenever I applied for a job, there I'd be, sniffling and sneezing, so no one would hire me. And of course that was the month the car decided to break down again – *(pauses)*

My kid and I were living on potato salad. Potato salad! It was the only thing I could afford to make and had the strength to make. Susan would cook and peel all the potatoes for me, then I'd chop them up and put all the seasonings in. I'd make about five pounds of it and shove it in the icebox. And we'd live on it for a week! Then I'd make another five pounds –

He: Hey – how's this? *(does a little jump and turn; or, if smoking a cigar, blows smoke rings)*

She: You're good! Ah, you know, to this day, I cannot look at potato salad. And then, if that wasn't enough, my kid needed a long-sleeved white blouse for graduation. And a dark skirt. And she didn't have either. And I just had no money left. There hadn't been a money order for years. So every night, I'd just curl up in bed and play back the old memories of Mike. The way the back of his neck looked when he was concentrating over that old white upright, hitting the keys –

He: What happened about your daughter's graduation? *(music fades)*

She: Someone's older sister had an old outfit. It didn't really fit Susan, but I told her, you do what you have to in this life.

He: Why the hell didn't you call Mike?

She: I never thought of it.

He: Didn't you think he would help you?

She: I didn't need his help.

He: You were out of work. Your child was practically starving.

She: She was stuffing herself with potato salad. We both gained five pounds. Look, I didn't even know Mike's address.

He: You couldn't find it if you really needed it?

She: I suppose so. You don't understand. I don't ask favors.

He: Favors? That was his child, too, in that hand-me-down graduation outfit.

She: Wait a minute. *(stands)* You better not be telling Sally Foster Rivers about raising her own child. Because I raised Susan myself without any help from anybody. And I did a damn good job of it!

He: I'm sure you did. But pride like that can be a kind of selfishness. You didn't give the man a chance.

She: The last person in the world that I would have ever asked for help was Mike Rivers.

She: I'm not bitter. But the man decided to go, of his own free will. He could have come back at any time in all those years. He didn't want to.

He: *(angry)* How do you know he didn't want to?

She: It's obvious! Because he didn't come back!

He: People don't always know what the hell they want!

She: I do.

He: Which makes you a superior person. But if a man knew that his child was living on potato salad, that his former wife was sick and out of work, that his child had to wear a hand-me-down graduation uniform, that man might be happy to come back and help and he wouldn't be doing anyone a favor. He'd want to do it!

She: I don't care what he wanted! I wanted a lover, not a Red Cross mission!

He: Well, who knows what would have happened if he came back?

She: Nothing was stopping him!

He: Maybe he was ashamed for walking out on you. Did you ever think of that? Or that he thought his daughter hated him? And why shouldn't she? Or that his former wife was re-married? Or had a rich boyfriend? Or just plain hated the sight of him? And maybe he spent his whole life trying to forget that he owed somebody something, and hadn't paid his debt?

She: Mike didn't owe me anything! Anyway, Mike was not like any of those things you're describing. He knew that I understood he had to leave. And that when it was over, it was over. And that I'd never make his child hate him.

He: You don't know what he thought!

She: And what are you? Some wonderful faithful husband of thirty-five years with five children and fifteen grandchildren? Who are you to judge me?

He: Oh, I'm not judging you. But you're so damn self-sufficient. A man might have expected one letter . . . just one . . . asking him to come back.

She: You don't know anything about Michael Rivers. Mike wasn't like other people.

He: What?

She: When they were moving my things out of my house. I was on the sidewalk taking a last look at the street. And he was walking towards me. With that way of holding his arms away from his body. Hair in his eyes. Sun on that young neck. Of course, when he came closer, I saw it wasn't him. Nothing like him, really. This kid was just another kid. Mike wasn't like other people.

He: Everybody's like other people. Including you, Sally. Because you did not "shake hands and say goodbye." *(She looks at him in silent shock, disbelieving.)* Sally, when I left you forty years ago, your eyes held such hurt, such pain, such fury, that I ran all around the world to get away from that memory. All these years, I thought you hated me. But just to get it straight – when I was packing my bags forty years ago, you were picking up everything in the room and delivering it to the region of my head, and telling me to get out and never come back, and throwing even the money I left on the dresser. And a chair after me, down the stairs. You're a marvelous woman, Sally Foster, but you did not shake hands and say goodbye. *(pause)* You look so wonderful, Sally. I can't tell you the relief that you don't hate me. And that you felt like that . . . watching me when I slept. I had no idea.

She: You don't tell people things like that. Ever.

He: Sally – I would have come back. I thought of coming back – *(starts toward her but she backs away)*

She: Your hair –?

He: How old was the kid you saw on the street today? Twenty-five? Twenty-eight?

She: You worked in a brewery!

He: About fifteen years ago, Janie died. Remember – the older sister I am supposed to have charmed? Well, I came back for the funeral. And – I needed a job. Harris had pull in the union. You never get the smell of the hops out of your clothes or your hair – but I was glad to have it. I'd been all over the world, but what I owned was on my back. Oh . . . I mean, you get the smell out after you leave the place . . .

She: Right here in town?

He: Did you think I was just going to wander forever? You know old Ben playing the sax on the corner? Now Ben could take any corner he wants. But he's always on the same corner. In front of the burger place. After a while, a man needs a sense of permanence.

She: You're not Mike. You might have known him. The voice isn't the same. Nothing. You're just an old man. I'm going upstairs.

He: And what about after the River Rats played all night and we'd go to the deli and take food to the park and eat at dawn? And Harris' girlfriend stumbling around in the grass in those crazy red high heels? And you wearing a gardenia in your hair like Billie Holiday?

She: You can't be Mike.

He: Sally. I won't pretend I've loved you all these years, but –

She: I'm sorry.

He: It's still me!

She: You sit in the park!

He: Not all the time! Christ, I wanted to have a drink for old Joe. Look, Sally, I remembered that cardinal in the snow for seventeen years. I loved that cardinal. A very red bird who made a magnificent image against the snow on a clear day in December. But it was just a goddam bird.

She: And you remembered him because he didn't turn drab and gray like everything else!

He: Sally! After all these years, are you just going to walk away from me?

She: I'm sorry! *(starts to exit)*

He: *(slumps on bench in defeat; shoulders sag, eyes go dull)*

She: *(seeing him slumped, is pulled back, hesitates, finally sits beside him)* It's freezing out here. Mike, feel that wind? *(to herself)* An old man with a wrinkled neck. *(Suddenly, he puts his arms around her. She falls against him.)*

BLACKOUT

Old Flames

by D. K. Oklahoma

Old Flames

by D. K. Oklahoma

Cast List
Angie Jimmy
Ray Henry
Ralph Grace

Old Flames

by D. K. Oklahoma

SCENE ONE

Time: The Present Place: A nice neighborhood in a small city. Set: The living room/dining room of Grace O'Riley's home. It is a "young looking" but comfortable room. A door, right, leads to the front porch. A doorway to the kitchen is stage left, and two more doors, center stage, a few feet apart, lead to the two bedrooms.

The flavor of the home is one of warmth, liveliness and energy. It looks lived in, with books, magazines, needlework and assorted bric-a-brac scattered about. A well-used pair of ladies jogging shoes is near one chair. A tennis racket is a in the corner and a stack of good records is beside the stereo. It is the kind of room that invites you to come in, prop up your feet and feel at home – but with style!

The doorbell rings, a multi-noted chime that plays "Hail, Hail, The Gang's All Here". There is no answer. The front door edges open and Angie's head appears.

Angie: Yoo-hoo! Anybody home? *(The door opens wider. Ray is disengaging his keys from the lock. Ray and Angie partly enter.)* Mother Grace? Yoo-hoo!

Ray: God's sake, Angie, don't call her that. You know she hates it. *(Calls out)* Mother? You home?

Angie: *(Methodically)* Grace, dear? It's Ray and An-gie. *(There is no answer. Their bright expressions fade and are replaced by worried, fretful looks. They enter and close the door.)*

Ray: *(Ruffling his hair)* Well, where the hell do you think she is? *(Peers around like a lost owl)* Why doesn't she stay home and watch soap operas like other old women.

Angie: *(meaningfully)* Now, Ray.

Ray: *(aggravated)* Angie, look, I really don't have time for this nonsense. Let's leave her a note and get out of here.

Angie: *(adamant)* Oh, no, you don't, sweetheart. You promised to talk to her. The car's in the drive, she can't be far. *(plunks down on the sofa.)* We can wait. *(Angie picks up a magazine and leafs through it. Ray taps his fingers, the pciture of a man waiting impatiently. Ray cleans his glasses, clears his throat several times, looks around.*

Ray: What time is it?

Angie: *(bored with his impatience)* 12:42

Ray: I hate waiting around like this. We should have called first.

Angie: I suggested that, remember? You wanted to look casual, as if driving 30 miles from the city could possible look "casual".

Ray: Well, it would have fooled her, she's not to bright. Want some gum? *(offers her a stick)*

Angie: No, thanks. How can you talk about your mother that way? That's not nice. *(Ray crams the gum into his mouth and chews busily for a moment. Angie ignores him. He paces a few steps.)*

Ray: *(briskly)* Well, *(beat)* enough of this. Let's look around.

Angie: *(displeased)* What.

Ray: *(chewing wildly)* You know, look around. If she's really got some man staying here, like old Mrs. Landers said, there's bound to be some sort of evidence, you know, a razor, shoes . . . clothes.

Angie: That's snooping!

Ray: So what? After all, she's my mother. *(getting pompous)* If she's gone off her rocker and gotten herself involved with some man, I've got to find out about it. It's my duty as her son to protect her from herself. *(draws himself up)* She many need counselling.

Angie: Oh, good grief. You are so stuffy! I don't know how a free spirit like Mother Grace ever raised such a hung-up son.

Ray: *(chews furiously)* I am not hung-up. I hate it when you say that.

Angie: *(archly)* "Physician, cure thyself!"

Ray: *(more heated)* And I really hate it when you say that. Just because I'm a psychologist, doesn't mean I'm supposed to be perfect. Ow! *(Ray grabs his face and whines.)*

Ray: I bit myself! *(Angie takes a tissue from her purse, and holds it out.)*

Angie: Again? Get rid of the gum.

Ray: I think I'm bleeding.

Ray puts his gum in the tissue, which Angie returns to her purse. Ray probes the interior of his cheek with a finger.

Angie: *(continues)* I know why you chew that stuff – classic oral regression.

Ray: Don't you talk about "oral regression"! You don't know anything about it! *(starts for the bedroom)* Get up. I'm going to see what I can find in the bedroom – you check out the guest room.

Angie: Ray, I'm opposed to this.

Ray: Angie, shup up and check it out. *(Ray heads for the bedroom as Angie goes slowly into the guest room. A moment passes.)*

Ray: *(offstage)* Oh, my God. I was right! He has moved in!

Angie: *(offstage)* There's a whole closet full of men's clothes in here! *(They emerge simultaneously from the two doors, each carrying a man's suit on a hanger. One is a very large suit – the other is much smaller.)*

Ray-Angie: *(simultaneously)* Look what I found! *(They suddenly compare the suits and suddenly discover the size difference. They look at each other in horror.)*

Ray: *(horrified)* Oh my God! She's got two of them!

Angie: *(very puzzled)* There must be a rational explanation for this.

Ray: *(very excited)* She's got two lovers!

Angie: *(very patient)* Ray, that's not rational! 67-year-old women do not go around having two lovers! There must be another explanation.

Ray: *(hysterical)* She's got two lovers, for God's sake! I knew it! She's gone berserk!

Angie: Calm down. Maybe it's not as bad as it looks.

Ray: *(clutches her)* Angie, I'm telling you – his stuff is all over her bedroom. The bedcovers are all rumpled up like . . . like . . . *(He shudders over the implications, unable to continue).*

Angie: *(pats him)* Now, now. Don't go all to pieces. Let's try to think this through. Maybe there's a reason . . .

Ralph: *(melodically,offstage)* Bunny face! Guess who's he-re? *(Ralph enters, carrying flowers. He sees Angie and Ray and recoils.)*

Ralph: *(startled)* Oh, my goodness. I'm looking for Grace O'Riley. The key fit . . . this must be the right house. *(He looks around.)* Where's Grace?

Angie: *(gets up)* It's the right house.

Ray: Who are you?

Ralph: A . . . er, a friend of Grace's. Who are you?

Ray: *(recognition dawning)* Her son. Wait a minute. Don't I know you?

Ralph: Her son? Little Ray-Ray? Well, I'll be damned. You grew up after all! I was sure someone would push you in front of a truck. Don't you recognize me? Ralph Davenport, your mother's ex-husband.

Ray: I knew it. Ralph Davenport. I thought you looked familiar. You seem smaller.

Ralph: *(thoughtful)* You seem taller.

Ray: I grew up.

Ralph: *(sourly)* So I see. *(nods at Angie)* And who's this pretty lady?

Ray: *(rattled)* My wife, Angie . . . uh, Angie, meet Ralph Davenport.

Ralph: Hello little gal.

Angie: Hello.

Ray: So – Ralph – what are doing here?

Ralph: *(annoyed)* There you go . . . starting with the questions already! Never could stand your questions. *(nastily)* I'm here because your mother invited me. That's why. *(Ralph shifts the flowers uncertainly.)*

Angie: *(reaches for flowers)* Could I put those in water for you . . .

Ralph: *(looking around)*Thanks. *(hands her the flowers)* Where is Grace, anyway?

Ray: We don't know. We're waiting for her, too. *(Ralph shifts a little uncertainly then makes a gesture of resignation. Angie starts for the kitchen.)*

Ralph: Well – guess I'd better get the rest of the stuff. It's still out on the curb. *(Ray and Angie exchange a look, Angie stops.)*

Ray: *(suspicious)* What stuff?

Ralph: My stuff, of course. The table saw's coming later – cross country express. I just brought mostly clothes and a few hand tools.

Angie: *(pressing him)* Then you've come for an, uh . . . extended visit? *(Ralph blushes, suddenly disconcerted.)*

Ralph: *(shyly)* Well, I guess so, if things work out . . . *(Angie suddenly remembers the unidentified suits, and decides it is her duty to try to hide them from Ralph.)*

Angie: *(to Ray)* Uh, Ray, dear . . . I'll go, uh, put these lovely flowers in water. Why don't you, tidy up a bit.

Ray: *(dense, as usual)* Huh? The place looks fine. What are you talking about?

Angie: Go hang up your suits, dear. *(to Ralph)* Then we'll help you with your things, Mr. Davenport.

Ralph: Ralph. Call me Ralph. That's real sweet, but I can manage. I'll be right back. *(Ralph exits. Ray grabs one suit and Angie the other. They start to rush them back where they came from, realize they are about to put the different size suits into the wrong rooms; they reverse and vanish briefly.)*

Ralph enters with a wheeled hand truck holding a suitcase and a variety of other cases. Ray is stunned at the amount of "luggage". Angie, headed for the kitchen with the flowers halts, string at the stack of cases. Ray and Angie exchange a look of dismay. Ralph parks the cart near the wall and takes inventory. Angie and Ray stare.

Ralph: Let's see, suitcase, sabre saw, quarter-inch drill, soldering gun, wrenches . . .

Ray: Good lord, you're a one-man fixit shop!

Ralph: *(nods proudly)* Yep. That's about the size of it. I can do almost anythin', needs doin'. I'm one of a vanishing breed. There's a big demand for a fellow like me. If the new freeway hadn't come along, I'd still be fixing things in Cleveland.

Ray: The freeway?

Ralph: *(uses his hands to demonstrate)* That's right. You see, the crazy city ran it right along side my shop and stuck the off-ramp right through my front door. Condemned the whole kit and kaboodle. After ten years in the same location. Pow! No more shop.

Angie: That's awful.

Ralph: *(philosophically)* Oh well, what the heck? Gotta have highways, I guess. Anyway, that's why I'm here – if Grace's garage works out.

Ray: *(stupidly)* The garage?

Angie: *(catching on)* Oh, my. Are you going to set up a new fixit shop in Mother Grace's garage? *(She makes a face of dismay at Ray.)* What an, uh, interesting idea . . .

Ralph: I can see who got the brains in your family, little gal, but how the hell does Grace let you get away with calling her that? Sounds like a blessed Mother Superior! *(cackles, somewhat like a dirty old man)* That's a good one! Especially in light of recent developments. *(Ralph continues to enjoy his private joke while Ray and Angie exchange uneasy glances.)*

Ray: *(concerned)* Er, exactly what "recent developments" are you referring to, Ralph?

Ralph: *(wags a jaunty finger at him)* Oh no, Ray-Ray, if Grace hasn't put you in the picture already, I'm not about to spoil her fun. I'll let her fill you in. *(consults his watch)* Say, where could she be?

Angie: You're sure she was expecting you . . .

Ralph: Oh, hell, yes. She sent me the key. *(holds it out)* See. I'm the last one.

Ray: *(suspiciously)* What do you mean . . . "the last one".

Ralph: *(coyly)* Oh, no you don't, Ray-Ray. Wait for your mother. *(Ralph picks up the suitcase and starts in the direction of the bedroom. Ray and Angie realize he is about to discover the other mens' clothing.)*

Angie: Oh, dear. *(Ray and Angie exchange panicky looks and Ray rushes to head him off. Ralph hesitates, oblivious to their actions, seems to remember something amusing, shakes his head ruefully and abruptly alters course toward the other bedroom. His action results in an unwitting evasion of Ray and Angie's attempt to intercept him. Ralph disappears briefly inside the bedroom.)*

Ray and Angie pantomime dismay, expecting a jealous outburst. Instead, Ralph emerges, completely unruffled, whistling, the very picture of a happy man. He rubs his hands together briskly.

Ralph: Well, wonder if Grace would mind if I raided the ice box? *(Ray and Angie, behind Ralph's back, make shrugging gestures. Maybe he didn't notice the other clothes. They are baffled.)*

Ray: *(absently)* Help yourself . . .

Ralph: Anybody else hungry?

Angie: No, thanks . . .

Ralph : Okay. Here, I'll take care of those while I'm at it. *(takes flowers from Angie and heads for the kitchen; Ralph heads for the kitchen. Angie clutches Ray.)*

Angie: *(whispers)* I just threw that suit on the bed. He couldn't help but see it! Why didn't he say something?

Ray: *(chewing wildly)* Your guess is as good as mine! *(dramatically pantomimes a man in deep throught)* I've got to think! *(Angie wrings her hands while Ray "thinks" for a minute. Then the front door opens and Jimmy backs into the room, carrying one end of a long plank. He is mildly surprised to see Ray and Angie.*

Jimmy: Oh, hello. Who are you?

Ray: *(Not at all happy to see another visitor)* What do you mean: "Who am I"? *(chews)* This is my mother's house. Who the hell are you?

Jimmy: *(jovial)* Don't tell me! You're little Ray-boy, all grown up! My, my, don't you know me?

Ray: *(groans)* Jimmy O'Riley?

Jimmy: *(booms)* In the flesh. Good for you, Ray-boy. Is your mother around?

Ray: Never mind that. What are you doing here – in this house? Mother divorced you . . . 20, 30 years ago. *(chews wildly as he glares at Jimmy)*

Jimmy: Thirty-five, but who's counting? I wonder where she went? I don't want to leave this outside.

Angie: What is it?

Jimmy : *(cagey)* It's a surprise. *(holds the board so they cannot see the other side)* I'll let Gracie tell you about it.

Ray: *(to Angie, chewing)* This is an even bigger mess than I thought.

Angie: *(to Ray)* Ray – what are they doing here? I don't understand what's going on. A person just doesn't invite two ex-husbands back under the same roof . . . do they? What on earth is your mother thinking of?

Jimmy: *(to Angie)* Say, watch out little gal. Our Gracie can do any damn thing she wants to. *(gives Angie a closer look, strokes his mustache and gives her a wolfish grin.)* Who the thunder are you, anyway? Don't tell me Ray-boy snookered a pretty gal like you into messin' around with him!

Ray: *(stuffily)* This is my wife, Angie.

Jimmy: *(still holding board)* Pleased to meetcha. *(shakes her hand warmly)*

Henry: *(off stage, calls out)* Hey! What's the hold-up?

Jimmy: Oh, my gosh. *(Moves farther into the room with the long board)* I forgot all about Henry. *(another elderly man appears at the other end of the board, a little miffed. He is much smaller and more frail than Jimmy. Some sort of cap is sticking out of his rear pocket and he has a pencil behind one ear.)*

Henry: This thing's not getting any lighter. What's going on?

Jimmy: Let's put it over here. (*Together the two old men prop the long board up against the wall so that no one can see what is on it.*)

Ray: (*twitching*) I can't stand it. You must be Henry . . . uh, Henry . . . (*he can't get the last name*)

Henry: (*shuffles over to shake his hand warmly*) Jones. Henry Jones. Right! I'd know those beady little eyes anywhere. You've got to be young Raymond Richard. Well, how the world are you my boy? Long time no see! (*pumps Ray's limp hand warmly Ray dumbly chews his gum, staring at Henry in disbelief. All of his childhood nemeses have now descended simultaneously upon him and he is unable to cope.*)

Angie: (*to Ray*) Another ex-husband? (*Ray nods weakly, unable to speak*) Oh dear, I've got to sit down. (*Angie sinks to a chair, staring at the new arrivals. Ray starts to put a new stick of gum into his mouth, realizes he already has one, hesitates then crams it in anyway. He stares at the old men rather like a watchful mouse in the presence of a hungry cat, chewing. Jimmy wipes his hands on a bandana. Henry rocks on his toes, beaming at Ray. Ralph emerges from the kitchen, a sandwich in his hand. He is very glad to see the other two men.*)

Ralph: Hello! Hello!

Jimmy: Well, look who's here!

The three old men greet each other cherrily, thumping backs, shaking hands, ad-libing welcomes. Ray and Angie watch limply. The little reunion ends as they realize that Ray and Angie are not in the right mood. The older men sober up and caucus, exchanging slightly worried looks among themselves.

Jimmy: Ut-oh.

Henry: (*whispers to the other men*) Looks like Grace hasn't exactly told Raymond Richard about the – uh, arrangement.

Jimmy: (*serious*) Looks like!

Ralph: (*to others*) What should we do?

Henry: I wish Grace was here.

Jimmy: We've got to say something. (*Uneasily, they move toward Ray and Angie. Henry takes Angie's arm and leads her toward a seat on the sofa, smiling sweetly at her worried face. Jimmy makes a little "shooing" motion toward Ray to make him follow along and sit down, too. Ray and Angie, seated on the sofa, look up at the three old men, waiting for an explanation. Ray continues to chew his stupid gum and occassionally twitch. He is very uncomfortable. For that matter, so are the old men. Henry speaks reassuringly.*)

Henry: (*nodding*) It's really a beautiful thing your mother' done, Raymond. You'll be very proud of her.

Jimmy: (*colluding*) Yes, a beautiful thing.

Ray: (*uneasily*) What thing? What has Mother done?

Angie: What are you all doing here . . . together?

Ray: I thought you moved away. *(suddenly suspicious)* Say, whose clothes are those in mother's room?

Jimmy: Mine.

Angie: And who's are those in Ray's old room?

Henry: Mine.

Ralph: *(explains)* I haven't unpacked yet.

Angie: Thank God. Where would she put you?

Ralph: Probably in Ray-Ray's old room, with Henry, for now.

Ray: Could you please quit calling me that? I always hated it!

Ralph: *(calmly)* I know. *(holds up a hand of apology)* Okay, I'm sorry. I shouldn't needle you. It's just that you were such a spoiled little kid. Used to drive me batty. But, I shouldn't hold that against you, now.

Ray: *(shocked)* I thought you liked me . . . all of you! *(In unison all three old men adlib and shake their heads emphatically "no".)*

Ray: *(petulent)* Well . . . you sure acted like it! *(Another emphatic headshake from the old men. Ray looks hurt and confused. He spits his gum out and puts it in a nearby ashtray, rather like a scolded child. Angie puts a protective arm around her husband.)*

Jimmy: *(spreads his hands)* We had to . . . you were Gracie's boy.

Henry: What else could we do? It was a package deal . . . you and Gracie.

Ralph: Your own daddy was dead, before you were even born. You needed a father's influence.

Ray: *(sulky)* What influence? It was more like having three Santa Clauses trying to out-do each other.

Henry: Well, I guess we did over-do it a little, now and then.

Jimmy: But we meant well.

Ray: *(accuses them)* I don't believe you'd think you just spoiled me to get on the good side of Mother. All three of you! Henry . . . you never could keep a job. Always day-dreaming! And you, Jimmy – always after the ladies. Even I knew that! *(Jimmy hangs his head.)* And Ralph – wrapped up in your gadgets. If a thing worked properly, you never paid any attention to it! *(Ralph nods, glumly.)* No wonder she got rid of you all!

The old men nod in sad unison, looking at each other with hang-dog expressions.

Jimmy: We deserved it.

Ralph: We didn't know how lucky we were.

Henry: Your mother is an angel.

Ralph: A princess!

Jimmy: Better than the three of us, put together!

Henry: Maybe that's what gave her the inspiration . . .

Angie: *(at the end of her patience)* What inspiration?

Henry: It's really a beautiful thing *(waxing lyrical)* just like the return of Spring!

Angie: What is?

Ralph: Oh, no. We'll let Gracie tell you all about it. *(to the other old men)* Say, you fellows want to help me get the rest of my stuff into the garage? I left it out front.

Jimmy: Sure, come on Henry.

Henry: You got much? *(The three men exit, adlibbing conversation about the tools, etc., ignoring Ray's adlibbed attempts to call them back to the subject. Very frustrated, he turns to Angie.)*

Ray: *(still twitching)* Why does she do these things to me? Just look at this mess! She's alsways screwing up my life . . . ever since I can remember! I was the only kid on the block with three step-fathers. It was horrible.

Angie: *(comforts him)* There, there. I know. You had a very traumatic childhood. *(Angie leads Ray toward the sofa, taking the suit from his hand. Ray continues to twitch and fidget.)*

Ray: *(whimpering)* All those husbands . . . always trying to be nice to me – they gave me wagons and candy and took me to the zoo. *(sobs)* Do you know how hard it is to pretend to get excited over a hippopotamus week after week? It was Hell! *(twiches)*

Angie: *(soothingly)* I know. I know. *(Ray flops full length on the sofa. Angie sits in the chair near his head in classic "psychiastrist" fashion. She makes a little teepee on her fingers and nods wisely, lips pursed, as he rambles on.)*

Ray: Birthdays were hell, too. I got three erector sets! *(twitches)* 3 monopoly games! *(twitches)* 3 of everything!

Angie: Go on.

Ray: *(whines)* Always too much of everything. It was all her fault. No matter what my mother did, she overdid it. Once she made five cakes in one day – "to get them out of the way" she said. *(twitches)* She was the same way about husbands. Too many of them. Her name changed so often I gave up introducing her. It was all just too confusing.

Angie: I see.

Ray: It turned me into a very peculiar child.

Angie: Mmmm.

Ray: *(poetically)* Grace loved everybody and everybody loved Grace. She was a candle flame in a world of moths. She still is.

Angie: Uh, huh.

Ray: *(sad)* No one really liked me for myself. They only put up with me because I was *(mimics)* "darling Grace's little boy."

173

Angie: Uh, huh.

Ray: I had no identity of my own. I was lost in the crowd around her.

Angie: Hmmm.

Ray: *(very sorry for himself)* Ralph wanted me to fix things, like he did. I was all thumbs, of course. Jimmy tried to teach me how to garden, but I kept pulling up my carrots to see if they were ready yet.

Angie: Oh?

Ray: *(childlike)* I tried to put them back . . . *(he looks to her for sympathy.)*

Angie: *(kindly)* Of course you did.

Ray: But it didn't work. *(pouts)* Henry was the worst! He wrote poetry and could recite yards of the stuff. I could barely rhyme moon and July.

Angie: *(looks puzzled)* You mean, moon and June?

Ray: *(in despair)* See what I mean? I was hopeless! : *(Angie nods in sympathy)* They could do anything! What did I have to offer? I couldn't do anything to make her proud of me. I was a total disappointment. *(Angie gets up and goes to kneel beside Ray. She pats him.)*

Angie: Don't say that. She adores you!

Ray: She likes everybody. It's her talent.

Angie: But you're her son – her only child. She loves you the most!

Ray: *(hopeful)* Do you really think so?

Angie: I know so. After all, she got rid of them, but she kept you! You won!

Ray: *(brightening)* I never thought of it that way. *(frowns)* You know, I was never really sure why she got rid of all of them. They never acted mad at each other. I don't remember a single fight. Not one.

Angie: *(impressed)* Well, that's pretty good! Most couples fight a lot. At least you didn't have to put up with that.

Ray: *(thoughtful)* No, that was one good thing. *(He spots the discarded suit and groans.)* But now, now, she's starting up all over again – and at her age. *(begins to break up)* I can't take it. I can't take it! *(hides his face in the pillow and drums his feet on the sofa)*

Angie: *(exasperated)* Oh, my gosh! Get a grip on yourself. *(The other men return, adlibing about Ralph's new shop. In a protective gesture, Angie tries to conceal Ray's tantrum from them. He manages to regain some sort of control and sits up, pouting. Angie tries to pretend nothing is wrong, but the old men are uneasily aware that there is tension in the air and halt, concerned.)*

Jimmy: They look a little upset.

Henry: Yeah.

Ralph: I guess we'd better tell them.

Jimmy: I guess so.

Ralph: Who wants to start? (*Jimmy shakes his head violently. He doesn't want to try.*) How about you, Henry? You got a way with words. You tell 'em.

Henry: Oh, my.

Jimmy: Yeah, You tell 'em, Henry.

Henry: (*smiles beatifically*) Well, it was this way: after my second wife passed on, her grown-up children put me in a nursing home. Said I was senile.

Jimmy: (*defends him*) He wasn't senile at all – just thinking.

Henry: (*explains*) I've always been like that. I'll be thinking about a poem I'm working on, and just go off into my own little world.

Jimmy: He really concentrates!

Henry: They didn't even try to understand!

Jimmy: Henry's a marvelous poet. He even wrote a poem about a cabbage.

Henry: (*fumbles at his pockets*) Would you like to hear it?

Angie: Well, yes . . . (*Ray makes an angry "not now" gesture to Angie.*) . . . a little later, maybe.

Henry: It's called "Leafy Fist of Green".

Jimmy: Henry thinks cabbages look like fists. (*he demonsrates*) See?

Angie: That's very, uh, clever.

Henry: That's what poets do, you know – see things differently – it's our mission in life.

Jimmy: That's right, Henry. It's a mission!

Henry: My second wife's children never understood that. Come to think of it, neither did she. Always yelled at me when I was trying to write. Maybe that's why I never finished my book.

Ralph: You'll have a good chance to do that now, Henry.

Henry: I know, it's a miracle!

Ray: (*suddenly alert*) Hey! Wait a minute! (*jumps up*) You three losers aren't expecting my mother to support you, are you?

Angie: Oh, dear!

Ray: (*draws himself up, threatening*) I'll have something to say about that! She's got just enough income for herself – no stray ex-husbands included! (*Ray takes a pugilistic stance, lower lip sticking out. Angie restrains him.*)

Jimmy: (*insulted*) Hold on, boy. Just a damn minute.

Ralph: (*insensed*) We're not sponging off our Grace!

Jimmy: I'd die first!

Henry: Me, too. I'd never do that!

Ray: *(attacks Henry)* Oh yeah? I remember when you never could keep a job!

Henry: That's all in the past. Everything's different now. I just never had the right kind of job before.

Jimmy: That's right!

Henry: *(with pride)* Now I do, the perfect job!

Ray: *(suspicious)* Doing what?

Jimmy: Grace figured it out for him. See Henry's a wonderful driver . . .

Henry: *(boasting)* Never had a wreck in sixty year. Never even got a ticket.

Angie: *(impressed)* Really?

Henry: That's right!

Jimmy: He's opened up a Senior Citizen taxi service. Got a special license from the Mayor.

Henry: See? *(He pulls the cap from his pocket and puts it on. It says "Taxi".)* Half-price fares for older folks only. Take 'em to the grocery store, movies, doctor and so forth. *(quotes)* "Drive safe and sure on every trip and maybe I will get a tip!"

Jimmy: Grace says all cab drivers are really philosophers, so Henry gets lots of stimulation for his poetry.

Henry: Only work three days a week – just enough.

Angie: *(A little dazed)* Sounds . . . perfect . . .

Ray: *(to Angie)* Hush.

Henry: *(to Angie)* It is perfect! I love it! I've written four good poems already.

Jimmy: One's about a cabbage . . . remember . . . I told you . . .

Ray: *(cuts him off)* Well, what about the rest of you? What are you doing?

Jimmy: *(bragging)* I got a big vegetable garden out back. Grace arranged for me to sell my produce to the health food store on Commerce. All organic. No chemicals. *(to Angie)* Onions'll be ready next week, want me to put you down for some? *(pulls out small notebook)* You can charge it.

Angie: *(He's winning her over.)* Uh, sure. Why not?

Jimmy: *(strokes his mustache and flirts with Angie)* I worked out a deal with a couple of cute old ladies on Fifth Street to home-can my surplus for us to eat next winter, if we have any left over. Nothin' beats home grown, home canned vegetables . . . *(Ralph gives him a knowing look thinking Jimmy is up to his old tricks again.)*

Henry: Jim always had a green thumb.

Jimmy: *(modestly)* Used to teach agriculture at the Vo-tech.

Ray: *(reluctant)* Well, I guess that sounds . . . all right . . . *(to Angie)* What do you think?

Angie: Sounds . . . very, uh, enterprising. Nobody uses that big back yard anyway.

Ray: *(gives a meaningful look at Ralph's tools)* And I suppose you're going to open a fix-it shop?

Ralph: Finally got it! I knew you were smarter than folks gave you credit for! *(Ralph, Jimmy and Henry all laugh at Ray's expense. Ray becomes a bit defensive and finds an excuse to break off this conversation. He looks at his watch.)*

Ray: *(to Angie)* This is taking longer than I thought. I've got to call my office. *(Ray starts toward the kitchen. Ralph has finished his sandwich and all but the last swallow of his milk as this scene progresses.)*

Ralph: Oh! Ray-Ray. Just a minute. *(Ralph motions Ray back, finishes the last swallow of milk, stuffs his paper napkin in the glass and hands Ray the empty glass to take to the kitchen. Ray snatches the glass and exits in a huff. The old men laugh.)*

Angie: *(conspiratorily)* Well, now gentlemen, this is all very nice . . . but what about your living arrangements? You aren't all actually living here, are you? Together? *(The three old men are now discomfited. Their bravado vanishes and they shift their feet uneasily, looking at teach other with embarassment, they would like to duck the whole issue.)*

Jimmy: Maybe you'd better discuss that with Grace. She explains things so much better. *(They all nod eagerly, anxious for an easy way out.)*

Henry: She'll tell you.

Ralph: Yeah . . . ask Grace, she'll tell you.

Angie: *(firmly)* I think you'd better tell me, now. *(points after Ray)* He's not going to give up until he gets to the bottom of this, you know Ray! *(They give up, look at each other and by mutual consent, push Jimmy forward as spokesman. Jimmy clears his throat, unable to really meet her eyes.)*

Jimmy: Well, you see, we, uh, all uh, loved . . . I mean love Gracie . . .

Ralph: I never got over her!

Henry: Me, either! She's the sweetest woman in the world. "Sweetness and rhythm in every motion, I offer Gracie my eternal devotion!"

Ralph: *(winces; to Henry)* Yeah, well . . . *(to Angie)* I've thought about her every day of my life – that's why I never remarried – never found anyone close to Gracie. I was such a fool to let her go!

Jimmy: *(eagerly)* Me, too! Why did I chase other women when I had Gracie? I must have been crazy. Now I know better! She was the best!

Henry: I wrote her a thousand letters and poems, begging to come back home, but, you know, I never got up enough nerve to mail any of them. I was afraid she wouldn't want me.

Jimmy: Look at it this way. Grace is a hell of a woman! Too much woman, in fact. None of us was good enough for her, by ourselves – that's why she got rid of us, and I don't blame her!

Henry: Me, either. I think she only married me in the first place because she felt sorry for me.

Ralph: I think she wanted to get me out of my shell – away from things and more with people. But I didn't try hard enough. I let her down . . . but now she's giving me another chance.

Henry: But none of us has to do it all alone! That's the beauty of it, don't ya see? *(quotes)* "All alone, we did fail, but now together, we'll prevail"! *(Ralph applauds the poem.)*

Angie: So how did you all get here?

Jimmy: It started a couple of months ago. I was living in a tiny little apartment in downtown Dallas – all I could afford. One dinky little window that opened onto an alley full of junk. I wrote to Grace one day and told her how bad I felt without a little dirt to dig in. She invited me to spend a few days here – said I could putter around the yard all I wanted to.

Ralph: That was the start. Jimmy just couldn't go back to that awful dump – Grace wouldn't let him. So he just stayed.

Henry: I was the next. After finding Jimmy, Gracie got to wondering what had become of me. She called my second wife's son and found out where they'd stuck me. I cried when I saw her sweet face in the visitor's room. I'm only 76, but I was ready to give up.

Jimmy: Grace packed his suitcase then and there and brought him home with us.

Henry: *(beaming)* She said they needed me. Can you imagine that?

Ralph: *(claps Jimmy on the back)* I got Jimmy to thank for calling me.

Jimmy: *(affectionately)* Oh, hell, Ralph – I just couldn't get that damn Rototiller to work. Then I remembered you and the way you got with mechanical stuff . . . and we always got alone pretty good . . . I was in a bind over losing my shop. I had all my stuff stored in an extra bedroom with no space to work. I was sure glad to hear from Jimmy. So here I am! *(Very distracted, Ray re-enters from the kitchen.)*

Ray: She put me on hold, my own secretary put me on hold!

Angie: She doesn't like you, dear, remember. But she's working on it. *(back to the others)* Now, gentlemen, this is all very nice, but it still doesn't answer my question. How are the four of you living here, in a two bedroom house?

Ray: *(remembers the problem)* Oh! Yeah! What the hell's going on here?

Angie: They were just about to tell me, dear. Now, what about that stuff in Grace's room?

Jimmy: *(backing off)* Tell 'em, Henry . . .

Henry: *(embarrassed)* Oh, dear. You tell them . . . you can . . .

Ray: *(angry)* Damnit! Somebody tell me! *(The other two push Jimmy forward to speak for them all. He takes a deep breath, mustering his courage.)*

Jimmy: *(very hesitant)* It's, uh, really very, uh, simple. You see, we, uh – take turns.

Ray: *(growing dismay)* Take turns? Doing what?

Jimmy: *(embarrassed)* Well, there were two of us . . . and now with Ralph, there'll be three . . . and anyway, there's, uh, only one, uh of Grace . . . so we just, uh, sort of, uh rotate – a week at a time.

Ray: *(hysterical)* You rotate? You mean you rotate taking turns with my Mother? Oh my God! my God! *(He tears his hair, tugs furiously at his tie, almost pulling it off, throws his jacket off one shoulder. He is wild-eyed.)*

Henry: *(calming him)* It's not as bad as all that!

Jimmy: Don't go all crazy on us – let us explain.

Henry: It's not just a matter of lust . . .

Ray: Lust! My God! Lust! You're talking about my Mother! Lust! My God! *(disarrays his clothing even more)*

Angie: *(amused now)* What are you doing here, anyway, playing musical beds?

Henry: *(giggles)* That's kinda cute.

Jimmy: *(to Henry)* I guess it does look sorta like that . . .

Ralph: *(grinning)* I never thought of it that way!

Ray: *(hysterical)* Well it isn't cute! It's disgusting! A senior citizen love-in!

Henry: *(mildly)* Well, remember Raymond Richard, everyone needs love.

Ralph: That's right.

Ray: *(shouting)* But not from my Mother! She's not up for grabs! This is a respectable woman!

Jimmy: Well of course she is! We wouldn't do a thing in this world to hurt Grace in any way whatsoever!

Angie: What will people think about all of you moving in here?

Ralph: If they even pay any attention, we hope they'll think it's a good idea.

Jimmy: I sure do!

Henry: No one outside the family knows where anyone is sleeping. It's none of their business. *(The old men all nod emphatically, looking at each other for moral support.)*

Jimmy: *(bravely)* As far as anyone else is concerned, this is strictly a business arrangement. I'm renting a room and the yard.

Henry: *(chimes in)* And I'm leasing the car and renting a room.

Ralph: And I'm renting the garage and a room.

Jimmy: It's purely business. *(smiles to himself)* Most of it!

Ray: *(plaintive)* But you're sleeping with my Mother!

Ralph: *(protests)* Not me. I haven't even unpacked yet!

Ray: *(attacks Ralph)* Well, it's probably only a matter of time! *(Ralph considers the idea, shrugs happily and grins.)*

Jimmy: After all, I used to sleep with her when we were married and nobody objected.

Henry: Me, too.

Ralph: *(sing-songs)* Yo!

Ray: You were married then. That was different.

Jimmy: *(slyly)* How do you know we're not married again? *(He rocks on his toes, grinning.)*

Ray: *(gasps, totally thunderstruck – He will believe anything at this point.)* Are you?

Jimmy: *(shrugs)* Nope. But how do you know we're not? And for that matter, how would anybody else know either? She's still using my name.

Angie: That's right. She is!

Ray: *(groans)* This is all so confusing. *(Sits down and buries his head in his hands.)*

Henry: Your problem, Raymond is that you're all hung up on sex. Sex isn't all there is to loving someone.

Ray: What are you talking about.

Ralph: Henry's right. I enjoyed a good back rub almost as much. Just because people are sleeping in the same bed, doesn't mean they're having sex.

Ray: *(glares at him)* Well, it's a pretty good indication.

Jimmy: *(sticks his tongue in his cheek and looks wise)* Only with some people . . . *(Ray glares at him.)*

Henry: I enjoy a nice snuggle the most – I really missed that part of marriage so much. There's no one to snuggle with in a nursing home. *(getting lyrical)* I felt like a withered corn stalk in the garden of life. I was just drying up for someone to hold.

Angie: *(tenderly)* I know just what you mean. I love it, too!

Ray: *(surprised)* You do? You never told me.

Angie: *(sadly)* I tried. You never listen. *(Ray gives her a long thoughtful look, almost forgetting about the others.)*

Henry: So . . . who cares if I snuggle up to Grace every other week or so?

Jimmy: It's nobody's business but ours.

Ralph: And Grace's!

Ray: But it looks . . .

Jimmy: *(interrupts)* It's really not even your business!

Ray: But you can't . . .

Henry: *(rather smug)* I think it's the perfect answer to all our problems. I'm real proud of us – all of us – for giving it a chance.

Ray: But what if . . .

Angie: But – won't you be jealous of each other? Have misunderstandings?

Ralph: *(shrugs)* Maybe.

Jimmy: *(booms)* Who cares? If we do, at least it's better than being all alone where nobody gives a damn what you do.

Ralph: Right!

Jimmy: *(joyful)* At least we'll have somebody to be jealous of – somebody to fight with . . .

Henry: . . . And somebody to fight over . . . our Gracie!

Jimmy: I feel like a kid again! Can't wait to get up in the morning.

Henry: Me, too!

Jimmy: There's somebody to share things with – I can smooch Gracie . . . and talk about the baseball game with Henry . . .

Ralph: *(interjects)* Football's my sport!

Jimmy: *(includes him)* And football with Ralph, now that he's here.

Henry: And I've got somebody to listen to my poems.

Ralph: *(to Henry)* And somebody to fix your typewriter, too – Grace told me you've got a sticky "S". *(laughs at his own corny joke, joined by the others.)*

Henry: *(remembering)* That's right! I lost my "s" right in the middle of typing a poem about the "rusty shell of a steam ship" It came out "the rutty hell of a team hip" – It just ruined the whole thing.

Angie: *(to Henry, trying to keep a straight face)* What a shame.

Ralph: I'll get right after it.

Ralph: I'll get right after it.

Jimmy: So you see, Ray-Ray, we're all going to help each other.

Ray: Well . . .

Angie: And Grace is happy about all this? *(The old men nod, looking at each other with rather coy little smiles. Jimmy strokes his mustache.)*

Henry: She certainly seems happy. She told us that not a day passed without her worrying about us and how we were getting along all alone.

Jimmy: That's right.

Henry: Now she can keep a eye on us.

Ralph: I worried a lot about her, too. It's hard for a woman to keep up with an old house like this.

Angie: That's right.

Ralph: Something's always breaking down or wearing out. She doesn't even know how to light the furnace.

Angie: *(to Ray)* That's right, Ray. You always have to come over and do it.

Jimmy: And that huge yard! Do you know what she was paying just to have the grass cut?

Angie: *(to Ray)* And remember last summer when the boy mowed right over her French lilac bush?

Jimmy: It's nothin' but a stub, but I'll save it. *(Ray looks uncertainly from one to the other, sofening a bit.)*

Henry: And Raymond Richard, you must know how she hates to drive a car. She never did learn how to park one straight.

Angie: Oh, me either.

Henry: So now, I do all the driving for her.

Angie: How sweet.

Ray: *(still doubtful)* I don't know . . .

Angie: Well, I do! I think it's a wonderful idea!

Ray: *(very surprised)* You do?

Angie: *(moves closer to the old men)* It's absolutely perfect, don't you see, Ray? They all mesh together!

Ray: *(sour)* I know – it's the "meshing" I object to! If only she were decently married.

Ralph: Why would she want to get married again? This way we've all got our independence.

Henry: And nobody gets left out.

Jimmy: And Grace gets the rent and food money.

Angie: *(to Ray)* I don't see how you can argue with that one!

Ralph: Don't forget kid – we're all old enough to be your father.

Jimmy: *(to Ralph)* What'd ya mean? We were his father! *(The old men share in the joke.)*

Ray: It's a little hard to get used to. I'm not sure I like the idea of you guys being back in my life – you used to drive me crazy.

Henry: You drove us crazy!

Jimmy: Always snooping around, asking a million questions. Wanting to know "why, why, why" about everything anyone did!

Henry: Private things that were none of your business.

Ralph: I never thought you'd grow up. Always thought somebody'd push you in front of a truck. *(beat)* Say, what kinda business did you go into, anyway?

Ray: *(proudly)* I'm a psychologist. *(The old men look at each other and nod wisely.)*

Jimmy: *(to the others)* It figures!

Ralph: We might've guessed!

Henry: *(to the others)* Now he gets paid for being snoopy!

Ray: *(protests)* It's not snooping! I have to ask questions so I can understand why people do things. So I can help them.

Ralph: *(sarcastic)* Uh, huh!

Henry: Sure!

Ray: *(whines)* I do! I help a lot of people.

Jimmy: *(dryly)* I'll bet!

Ray: *(a pouty baby)* I do! People come to me with all sorts of problems – loneliness, drinking, frustration, lack of purpose in life. I help them work out practical solutions.

Jimmy: *(on the trail of something useful)* And what sort of advice do you give your patients?

Ray: *(very serious)* I tell them to stay active, be with friends, do useful work . . .

The old men look meaningfully at each other making adlibs and gestures as if to say, "That's exactly what we're doing here". Ray finally realizes where this is leading and takes a defensive stance, aware he is being backed into a corner.

Ray: *(hostile)* Oh, no you don't! You're trying to trap me! This is not the same thing at all!

Henry: *(pressing the point)* Oh, no? I felt so useless and lonely I wanted to die – until Grace rescued me!

Jimmy: And I was hitting the bottle pretty regular in that dumb apartment. Haven't touched a drop since I got back with Grace.

Ralph: And me, I was so frustrated! Didn't know what the hell to do with myself. I had all those tools and no way to use them.

Angie: *(to Ray)* I think they got you, this time, big boy!

Ray: *(to Angie)* Whose side are you on, anyway?

Angie: Who says I have to take sides? I think we should all be on the same side.

Jimmy: Good for you, doll!

Angie: It looks to me like these folks of yours have come up with a pretty good scheme. It might not work for other families, but . . .

Ray: *(interrupts)* Don't call them a family!

Angie: What else can I call them?

Ray: *(angry)* A bunch of nuts!

Jimmy: *(to Henry)* He always was a brat.

Ralph: Why didn't one of us push him in front of that truck?

Henry: *(to Ralph)* Only because Grace wouldn't like it.

Ray: Cut that out! Maybe you are a family – sort of – but you're not my family!

Jimmy: *(adamant)* Who the hell cares? All I care about is Grace – and now of course Ralph and Henry, too. If we stick together, everything's gonna work out just fine.

Henry: It's like a second chance. A new home. A new family. I always wanted to have brothers.

Ralph: Me, too! *(pounds Jimmy on the back)* Somebody to crawl under the car with!

Angie: I think they've got a point, Ray. After all, who is this going to hurt?

Angie: I think they've got a point, Ray. After all, who is this going to hurt? I know Grace has been lonely. How often do we get over to see her? One day she got to reminiscing about the old days and she told me how much she missed them all. She calls them her "old flames". *(Henry adlibs, "That's us!")* She was worried about how they were getting along, now that they're older. She said she wished they lived closer so she could keep an eye
on them.

Ray: *(sourly)* This is closer, all right.

Angie: After all, Ray, it's none of our business how your mother runs her private life, as long as she's well and happy? At her age, why shouldn't she do as she pleases? Like Jimmy says, they are all grown-ups!

Ray: Sometimes you surprise me. I had no idea you were so *(with distaste)* so . . . liberal.

Angie: As a matter of fact, I think it's a great idea! They can all look after each other. *(meaningfully)* Less worry for you, too . . . about the house and all. *(gives him a little nudge)*

Ray: *(gets the idea)* Well, I always did worry about Mother's driving . . .

Henry: Not any more!

Angie: And you won't have to worry about fixing things, either, not with Ralph around.

Ralph: You tell him, sweetheart!

Jimmy: And you sure as hell won't have to worry about her being lonely!

Ray: *(snorts)* Humpt!

Angie: Well, I, for one, am delighted – now that I've thought it over. I think you should be, too, Ray.

Ray: *(sulking)* Humpt.

Angie: *(to Ray)* Come on, admit it. Your mother is going to be a lot happier now that her "old flames" are all back home.

Henry: Come on, Raymond Richard, wish us good luck in our new business.

Jimmy: Be a sport!

Ralph: Yeah! Remember when I helped you build your lemonade stand? Wish us good luck.

Angie: That's right, Ray. This is just like a mini-conglomerate. Henry's taxi service, Jimmy's produce business and Ralph's fixit shop.

Ray: *(scarcastic)* Yeah. Grumpy, Dopey and Mr. Fixit visit Snow White and *(with emphasis)* "whistle" while they work!

Angie: Ray! Cut that out!

Jimmy: I'm ashamed of you, Ray-boy!

Ray: *(to Jimmy)* Please don't call me that!

Angie: *(to Jimmy; hoping that if she ignores Ray, he'll get with the program)* Have you picked a name for your new, uh, business?

Jimmy: Of course. There was only one thing we could call it that would reflect the true spirit fo the venture. Henry thought it up.

Henry: It was unanimous.

Ralph: I voted by phone.

Angie: Well . . . what is it? I'm dying to know!

Henry: *(points to board)* Jimmy painted us a nice sign to put up in front of the house.

Ray: *(weakly)* You can't do that in this neighborhood.

Henry: *(unruffled)* Yes, we can. No problem at all, as long as we don't attach it to the house.

Jimmy: We're going to put it up on the lawn right in front of the porce, on stakes.

Angie: *(points to board)* Well, aren't you going to show it to us?

Henry: Why not? *(Henry and Jimmy get the board and carry it to the sofa, accompanied by adlibs, "Are you ready?" "Be careful," "You're gonna love it!", etc. They turn it over and set it across the arms of the sofa so that the audience can see the lettering. The sign says: "The Amazing Grace Family Co-Op. Natural vegetables, home repairs, taxi service".)*

Angie: *(claps)* Oh, I love it! *(She gives Henry a little kiss.)*

Ray: *(throws his hands up in disgust)* I give up. You've thought of everything. You people do whatever you want. I won't interfere.

Jimmy: Good.

Henry: You won't be sorry. *(quotes)* "Just leave us alone to do our thing and you will hear the birdies sing!"

Ralph: I'm proud of you, boy. *(Angie hugs Ray and kisses his cheek with warmth. She is very proud of him. Like the stuffed shirt he is, Ray fends her off, but she is too pleased to care. From outside the front door we hear a woman's bright, musical voice. We just know that voice belongs to a lovely person.)*

Grace: Yoo-hoo! I'm home. Is anybody here?

Ray: *(sadly)* Everybody's here!

Jimmy: It's Grace. It's about time.

Henry: Oh, good. Now we can really get going.

Ralph: *(combs his hair quickly)* I can hardly wait to see her!

They all turn expectantly toward the front door as the . . .

Curtain Falls.

Bonnie L. Vorenberg, MS., Theatre, is the Founding Director of *Arts for Elders* and the Artistic Director of the *Oregon Senior Theatre Ensemble*. Since 1979, she has provided arts education for seniors including classes in acting, dance movement, theatre appreciation and theatrical production. The *Oregon Senior Theatre Ensemble* performs on a regular schedule to audiences of all ages throughout Oregon and Washington. They were the only senior performing group to be selected to represent Oregon at Expo '86. The work of *Arts for Elders* and the Ensemble has been documented at state, regional and national conventions, and in numerous television, newspaper and journal articles.

Ms. Vorenberg is the author of *A Guide to 49 New Plays for Senior Adult Theatre*, a practical handbook *Enriching An Older Person's Life Through Senior Adult Theatre* and numerous articles.

Ms. Vorenberg has served on the Portland-Multnomah Commission on Aging and on the National Senior Adult Theatre Committee of the American Theatre Association. She is the National Enrichment Director for Brim & Associates, Inc., the nation's largest owner/operator of retirement homes. Ms. Vorenberg is often called upon to speak at conferences and to present workshops. She has become a nationally recognized spokesperson on arts and aging.

New Plays for Mature Actors is typeset in extra large twelve point type to make the text widely accessible to readers with limited vision. Exceptionally readable Palatino roman and italic typefaces are employed for the text and stage directions. San serif Eras bold and ultra typefaces distinguish character names, and page headings from the text.